Not Only the Market

NOT ONLY THE MARKET

The Role of the Market, Government, and
the Civic Sector in the Development of
Postcommunist Societies

Martin Potůček

CEU PRESS

Central European University Press
Budapest

First published in Czech as *Nejen trh. Role trhu, státu a občanského sektoru v proměnách české společnosti*, by Sociologické nakldatelství Praha, 1997.

English edition published by
Central European University Press

Október 6. utca 12
H-1051 Budapest
Hungary

400 West 59th Street
New York, NY 10019
USA

Translated by Therese Buchmeier
Translation supported by Local Government and Public Service Reform Initiative
(Affiliated with the Open Society Institute)

© 1999 by Martin Potůček
English translation © by Martin Potůček 1999

Distributed in the United Kingdom and Western Europe by
Plymbridge Distributors Ltd., Estover Road, Plymouth PL6 7PZ, United Kingdom

ISBN 963-9116-52-1 Cloth
ISBN 963-9116-51-3 Paperback

Library of Congress Cataloging in Publication Data
A CIP catalog record for this book is available upon request

Printed in Hungary by Akaprint

TABLE OF CONTENTS

LIST OF TABLES

PREFACE TO THE ENGLISH EDITION

I am very happy that this book has at last found its way to the English-speaking community. I believe that many of the societal and regulatory problems faced by the Czech Republic since 1989 are common to other countries—especially those of Central and Eastern Europe.

I am always appreciative of the opportunity to learn about additional potential applications of the concepts put forward in this book. Comparison is always fruitful as it often leads to both better understanding and a more solid basis for criticism. For this reason, I would urge readers not to hesitate to share their insights with me.

I would like to pay tribute to the Local Government and Public Service Reform Initiative (affiliated with the Open Society Institute) which has generously supported the English translation and facilitated the publication of this book.

PREFACE TO THE CZECH EDITION

I wrote this book because I had to. I do not mean that anyone forced me to do it. The first several years of societal rebirth in the Czech Republic since 1989, however, have been filled with so many events and changes—and, at the same time, with so many explanations as to why they happened—that I could not leave them unexplored, either as a sociologist or as a citizen. I have become increasingly aware of the meagerness of the many interpretations that have been presented to the public in newspapers, on television, in politicians' speeches, and even in the pages of academic journals.

The second significant motivation for writing this book was the efforts of Václav Havel, President, first of Czechoslovakia, then, since 1993, of the Czech Republic, to encourage a dialogue concerning desirable visions for Czech society: collective considerations about worthwhile goals, what Czech society should seek to achieve, what it should support, and what it should avoid. Along with President Havel, I am convinced that such an effort is important and should be attended to not only by professional politicians, but also by all citizens who are interested in public affairs. Such a dialogue has not developed in the Czech Republic—as a country we are still not focusing on creating the foundations of an open society along the lines laid down by Karl Popper (1994). This is a frustrating state of affairs and, unfortunately, not an unfamiliar one. What is especially frustrating is that, after fifty years of communism and during the important societal rebirth we are currently experiencing, the chances of effecting such changes based on the desires and dedication of a majority of citizens are significantly higher than they would be in circumstances of relatively stable development, such as those typical of many countries to the west.

The Czech Republic is faced by nothing less than a 'choice of society'. By 'choice of society' I understand, along with Roebroek (1992), the establishment of the main regulators of societal life—those which fundamentally influence the motivations and behavior of people and institutions, and, as such, create the prerequisites for democratic society to proceed in a particular direction. One function of public policy is to seek proportionality, balance, and effectiveness in setting the basic regulators, such that actions which conform to the conditions set by those regulators are aimed towards goals considered desirable, legitimate, and generally beneficial to a given society within a given period of time.

Understandably, politics cannot be all-powerful in this sense; public policy can inspire, create, and form a society, but it cannot go farther than is allowed by social traditions, norms, and culture. Mikhail Gorbachev, for example, was not successful in Russia mainly because the 'cure' of democracy as prescribed to Russian society was too radical—people were not prepared for it. The ability of public policy to inspire and realize particular visions of society, on the other hand, should not be underestimated. This is shown by the case of Germany after the Second World War. Under the trusteeship of the Western Allies, it emerged from the ruins of Hitler's defeated fascist state to become the Federal Republic of Germany, which today is one of the most robust European democracies.

The situation in Czech society has occasionally induced me to express my opinions in the pages of newspapers and academic journals. However, under the pressure of smaller and larger daily muddles, affairs, and emergencies, the ensuing dialogues more or less wasted away. More and more—and from many perspectives—these discussions seemed to fall on deaf ears: economists, philosophers, sociologists, political scientists, and lawyers, all utilized their own paradigms and intellectual *clichés* to prove they could manipulate the conceptual apparatus of their disciplines, and, in fact, they seemed able to grasp only a small part of the problems at hand (in this case, the exception proves the rule). Political journalists were maneuvering at an even lower level—as was political practice itself, more often than not. In these situations numerous examples of ideological 'dead wood' and/or lack of understanding, as well as distorted or mistaken interpretations of fundamental problems of the 'life-world', are clearly visible. The interest-group bias present in such interpretations may benefit only one segment of society. Nevertheless, both the decision-makers and those affected by their decisions are disoriented and misled to a degree which is often intolerable. Brzezinski (1993) warns strongly of the dangers of governments becoming ideologically entrenched rather than drawing conclusions based on careful analysis of development needs, threats, and advancement opportunities when applying their policies. According to Brzezinski, the rebirth of what he calls "meta-myths" would lead to the alienation of social consciousness from its real, living form.

My aim in writing this book is to offer readers an impartial analysis of the three fundamental regulators of society: the market, government, and the civic sector (non-profit organizations). I am interested not only in their strengths and shortcomings, but also in their mutual dependencies, the viability of alternative or complementary applications, and the particular practical problems to which they are more, less, or not at all suited. Their more exact definition will be the subject of the first section of the book. Here I will only point out that, although I understand these three sectors as keys to the realization of every specific 'choice of society', they are not the only regulators influencing the life of society. Other important regulatory functions are performed by, for example, the family, other informal groups, and value systems.

Rose and Haerpfer (1992, 53) point out that the ongoing changes in Central and Eastern Europe constitute a significant opportunity for testing alternative social-science theories about political, economic, and social systems. I would add that these countries also constitute laboratories for testing meta-theories which attempt to analyze how social reality is affected by all of these systems at once. The present study is intended as a contribution to building a foundation for one of the many possible meta-theories which explain societal change, specifically in analyzing the influence of the market, government, and the civic sector. I put my theories to the test by critically examining the extent to which they explain the experiences which are transforming Czech society.

Let me assure the reader of my concern that such an analysis should strive to avoid ideological contamination. To some, anyone who does not support the market at all times and at any cost is a confirmed socialist, if not a communist agitator; to others, anyone who does not believe that government intervention can cure any social ill is a hopeless liberal,[1] if not an imperialist lackey. Primitive opinions of this kind have cost the Czech Republic too much for us ever to allow ourselves to be oppressed by them again. It is certainly worthwhile to discuss and disagree about the aims of society; nevertheless, it should be possible for a majority of participants to agree on a common denominator in respect of those aims (indeed, in a democracy this is essential). After that, making decisions about the extent and method of utilizing the market, government, and the civic sector to achieve those goals will be simpler. Social scientists should play a significant role in this 'technical' phase (after all, we would probably not object to engineers determining the optimal slope of a highway or zoologists selecting the ideal components of animal feed). Even so, there remains a significant opportunity for research, experimentation, painful errors, and costly remedies in the realm of public affairs.

This study is a combination of theoretical explanations and descriptions with interpretations of concrete public-life situations in the Czech Republic—and to a certain extent in other Central and Eastern European countries—since 1989. I have tried to develop and explain theoretical points, while at the same time applying theories to examples of situations that the people of this region have experienced, thereby placing the theoretical concepts in a more accessible framework. For this reason I have tried to eliminate specialized terminology whenever possible, resorting to it only where needed to avoid a distorted explanation. This book also contains theoretical passages, although only where I would be unable to explain real-life situations without them. In all these ways I have tried to make this study accessible to the non-specialist with an interest in public affairs.

The first section of the book is dedicated to a detailed analysis of the effects of the market, government, and the civic sector on each other and on society. Citizens bring their own preferences and activities to bear on the often unbalanced interrelationships of these systems. Their values grow from the historical experiences and cultural traditions of their country, as well as from living conditions and experience, and are influenced by political ideologies.

In the second section I examine themes whose explanation is founded upon identification of the specific regulatory role of the market, government, and the civic sector (or their absence and the resulting socially pathological phenomena). Specifically, I deal with the process of privatization, the role of corporatism in political life, and the problems of corruption and the Mafia. I also analyze the ability of public policy to define the role of specific societal regulators, as well as how they are applied and interrelated. However, I do not deal with politics as a struggle for political power, but rather as public policy, that is, how and why it does or does not express, acknowledge, and satisfy heterogeneous public interests.

In conclusion, I would like to return to my original motivation for writing this book. On the basis of the information collected and documented here I have attempted to show that government, the civic sector, and even individual citizens have suffered because theoreticians and politicians—specifically, the protagonists of neo-liberalism—have conceived and implemented the introduction of the market as the main, if not the sole, aim of societal transformation. Václav Klaus, Prime Minister of the Czech Republic between 1992 and 1997, was doubtless the most influential propagator of this theory and its associated policies, but he was certainly not alone. In this clarified perspective, I would like to begin a discussion about the 'choice of society' in the Czech Republic. Hopefully this book will also play a role in shaping similar discussions in other Central and Eastern European countries.

Popper, in his intellectual autobiography (1995), notes: "Always keep in mind that it is not possible to speak such that you prevent misunderstanding; you will always find someone who misunderstands you."

I present this book to its readers with the assurance that I have tried to minimize the scope for misunderstanding. I welcome all carefully considered criticisms of my opinions and conclusions.

ACKNOWLEDGMENTS

This study is the result of a three-year research project funded by the Grant Agency of the Czech Republic No. 403/94/0393, *Analýza procesu formování a realizace veřejné politiky České republiky po roce 1989* (An analysis of the process of public-policy formation and implementation in the Czech Republic since 1989). Background research for this publication was supported by the Research Support Scheme of the Higher Education Support Program, Grant No. 37/1995, and published as *Market, Government, and Civic Society in the Post-Communist World*. It has also been published in Czech, by means of Grant No. 403/96/0314 of the Grant Agency of the Czech Republic, as *Vydání dvou monografií k problematice veřejné a sociální politiky v České republice po roce 1989* (Two monographs on the problems of public and social policy in the Czech Republic since 1989). Many thanks to all of the abovementioned institutions for their generous support.

This study would not have been possible without the direct and indirect support of many people. I am indebted mainly to colleagues and friends who have worked with me to research public policy in the Czech Republic, particularly Miroslav Purkrábek, who coordinated this research, Josef Vavroušek, who was killed tragically in 1995, and Petr Háva, Head of the Department of Public and Social Policy at the Faculty of Social Sciences at Charles University, Prague. I greatly appreciate the long-term support of Miloslav Petrusek, former Dean of the Faculty of Social Sciences at Charles University, who supported our department as we sought a new direction in teaching and researching public policy. My colleague Lubomír Mlčoch, an institutional economist, and I debated issues surrounding privatization in the Czech Republic, and I gained much from numerous discussions with Brack Brown of George Mason University in the United States, an enthusiastic observer and analyst of public-policy development in the Czech Republic since 1989; with Richard Scheffler of the University of California at Berkeley, a health economist and public sector specialist; and with Diego Gambetta of Oxford University, a specialist on problems of the Mafia. Ladislav Blažek, Taisie Čebišová, Ivan Gabal, František Pavel Novotný, and Milan Sojka contributed useful suggestions on the working draft of this study. I was also inspired by informal discussions with Fedor Gál on the problems of public life in the Czech Republic. Stimulus and inspiration in my work have also come from frequent contact with my masters and doctoral students of public and social policy at Charles University.

The English version of this book was produced by Therese Buchmeier, one of many young Americans who have dedicated their energy and capabilities to the transformation in Central and Eastern Europe. Working with her has always been enjoyable, both during the translation of this book and in realizing the Parliamentary Internship Initiative and the Senate Internship Program, which have enabled Czech university students to contribute to the work of our Parliament.

My wife, Ivana Potůčková, deserves the highest praise, not only for the wonderful family environment she has created, but also for her constructive criticism concerning how to make this book more comprehensible to readers who are not specialists in the social sciences.

My sincere thanks go to all of these people.

I. THEORETICAL FRAMEWORK

1. Definitions of Terms and Their Interrelationships

1. Market, Government, and Civic Sector as Regulators of Human Activities

To begin with, let us examine whether it is necessary to regulate human activity, and if so, why. Although many people believe it is indispensable, conversations with anarchists who truly believe in that political philosophy quickly illustrate that not everyone feels the same. In fact, would it not be much more pleasant if one did not need to take into account the law, the necessity of making a living, of paying rent and membership fees?

The answer to this question is simple. People would quickly lose their enthusiasm for such freedom because these liberties would cause the collapse of the majority of social institutions that ensure the conditions for survival. Like it or not, contemporary social, economic, and political institutions are interconnected in such complicated and mutually interdependent ways that the regulation of human activity is a necessary condition of a society's survival and its members.

Regulation represents the creation of living conditions—material, legal, cultural, and ideological—such that it is possible to encourage desirable behavior. Regulations result from particular notions about the motivations of human behavior. They can have a directive character, as in a ban or requirement, or can be based on indirect instruments, such as the threat of sanctions or positive stimulation in the form of satisfying a particular need or providing a reward. Another form of regulation is training by the family and other societal institutions—including schools and churches—to internalize socially accepted and preferred behavioral values and norms.

Lindblom (1977) suggests that the functioning of global societies should be analyzed on the basis of definitions of the following elementary political and economic mechanisms (regulators) which influence and condition human lives and societies: (i) government as the expression of political power; (ii) the market as a medium of exchange; and (iii) education (indoctrination). Typical agents of indoctrination are educational systems and the mass media. Indoctrination can have a political motive (often guided by a specific ideology) or an economic motive (advertisement). Producers and mediators may find themselves in situations in which it is in their personal interest to give partial, biased, or distorted information.

Streeck and Schmitter (1985) state that the social sciences traditionally present community, the market, and government as the key mechanisms for maintaining social order. The authors point out, however, that this list is incomplete and add another category: associations (Table 1.1).

Table 1.1 Models of Maintaining Social Order

Regulatory model	Regulatory principle	Specialized scientific discipline
Community Market Government Associations	Spontaneous solidarity Competition Hierarchical control Harmonization through organization	Sociology Economics Law, political science Organizational theory, sociology of social movement

The Wolfenden Commission (1978) suggested that regulators should be classified in accordance with the schema presented in Table 1.2.

Table 1.2 Types of Sector Regulating Human Activity

Private informal sector	Private commercial sector
Government	Civic sector (Non-profit organizations)

The advantage of both suggested classifications is that they differentiate between the private informal sector—including family, neighborhood, informal groups, and community—and the civic sector, which consists of associations and non-profit organizations. (The definition of family as a regulating element in relation to government and the market was used by Možný in characterizing Czechoslovak society over recent decades (1991).) Most other studies place all of these items within the more general category of civil society (Archer, 1994). The difference is substantial because the above-mentioned organizational structures significantly distinguish non-profit organizations from the private informal sector, a fact still overlooked by most economic and political science texts.

Besides the regulators identified by Lindblom, Streeck and Schmitter, and the Wolfenden Commission, we should not omit another sphere which is central to both ethics and social philosophy: values and norms. This sphere is narrowly defined in terms of morality, value orientation, and cultural patterns of behavior pertaining to individuals and entire societies. The problems of value orientation and political ideologies as means of indoctrination are dealt with in more detail in chapters 5 and 6; however, it is worth noting that this study concentrates particularly on three of the above-mentioned regulators: the market, government, and the civic sector. What are their characteristics; how are they distinguishable; in what ways do they influence human living conditions and activities; on what suppositions of human characteristics are they founded; and how do they complement or clash with one another?

2. Preliminary Definitions of Market, Government, and Civic Sector

2.1 The Market

The market is a self-regulating system in which supply and demand, in association with profit and loss, allocate scarce resources more efficiently than any other known regulatory mechanism. The market mechanism is based on a voluntary agreement between seller and buyer to exchange a particular good or service. Balanced price systems, which regulate both production and consumption, are created on the basis of millions of such exchanges.

Prices generated by the market act as signals which are used as guides to maximize individual profit with the minimum expenditure of available resources. Regulation by means of the market, therefore, is based on the assumption that individuals attempt to maximize their own gain to the extent that the market makes it possible. Individuals or institutions pursue only their own egocentric interests. According to Adam Smith, the magic of the "invisible hand" of the market is based on the belief that collective satisfaction is attained through the pursuit of purely selfish interests and that society profits from the egocentric behavior of individuals. From this model of human behavior the theories of neo-liberalism are derived (Friedman, Buchanan, and to a certain extent Hayek) which purport to provide a universal model to explain human motives and activities. "Homo-economicus, rationalistic, isolated and preoccupied with self-interest, is but one offspring of the Man of Reason; the offspring has a neoclassical psychological sibling. The sibling, too, is largely reactive, driven by inputs, is without personality, hedonistic and egotistic, a-social, devoid of affect (or emotions)" (Etzioni, 1995, 89).

The market is affected by public administration and the exercise of political power. Laws protect personal freedom—including the right to enter freely into market relationships and to conclude purchase and employment contracts—and private property. Political power is, in this way, a prerequisite of an effective market. Other prerequisites of market functioning are values and norms which are clear to all participants. All of this together creates a social 'capsule', which is, "therefore, best considered an intertwined set of normative, social and governmental mechanisms which each have a distinct role but also can, within limits, substitute for one another" (Etzioni, 1995, 213).

2.2 Government

While the market is the medium of economic power, government traditionally creates a general societal framework and, at the same time, forms and exercises political power. According to the concept developed by Max Weber, government is ideally an impersonal representative and executor of what is declared to be the public interest or common good. The characteristics of a particular political system influence how the public interest or common good is determined and satisfied. In democracies the majority decides—although today even the majority's decision-making power is limited by postulates and codes which prevent the violation of the basic rights and freedoms of individuals and minorities. Under authoritarian regimes the rights of individuals are usurped by a narrow power elite.

A democratic government has recourse to three basic instruments in its regulatory activities: (i) the legal system, (ii) public administration, and (iii) fiscal policy (which allocates money from the public budget). In addition to these instruments an authoritarian regime may also have recourse to violence (democracies may also do so under particular extraordinary circumstances defined by law). In both cases, especially that of authoritarianism, ideological indoctrination is another important regulatory instrument.

The government regulates individuals' activities by means of generally binding legal codes and established penalties within the framework of a hierarchical punitive model. It also helps people in situations they are not capable of handling alone, by means of public social services—a client-centered model of administration (Hendrych, 1992; Potůček, 1995a; Večeřa, 1993). It may, therefore, be said that contemporary government is based on a model in terms of which human beings are sometimes managed by forcing them to pay penalties or by threatening their benefits, and at other times by positive reinforcement as a more effective means of control.

Although there is dissension about the optimal size and strength of government, it is useful to define and differentiate its basic functions: the general execution of political will in a given society—either directly through state administrative bodies or mediated by other empowered institutions (executive branch); the creation of laws (legislative branch); and the administration of justice by means of the legal system (judicial branch). After the trauma of two world wars, during which the government apparatus was abused for inhuman aims, an additional independent function was added which in some ways supersedes the others: the protection of basic human rights and freedoms. Government's other functions include the following, encompassing both the more or less indisputable and the more controversial: monetary policy and development of the banking sector; macroeconomic policy, that implements fiscal and other policies which make it possible for the economy to protect or develop production capabilities; internal and external security; development of transportation and communications networks; and environmental, education, social, and health care policy.

Government functions by means of its organs at the central, regional, and local levels. Parliament constitutes the legislative branch of government power. It may also be understood as the link which mediates between citizens and government. Through this mediator, citizens and government participate in the implementation of determinate administrative activities by means of autonomous organs, especially at the regional and municipal levels.

2.3 The Civic Sector

To begin with a terminological remark, in addition to the term 'non-profit organizations'—most commonly used to refer to organizations in this sector and the one used in this book—a number of other terms are used to designate organizations operating within the civic sector, such as 'non-governmental organizations' (NGOs) and 'civic associations' or 'initiatives'. The whole area in which these organizations function is generally called the 'civic sector' (Brown, 1994), as well as the 'non-profit', 'non-governmental', or 'third' sector.

The civic sector consists of organizations that take the form of voluntary citizens' associations with common values and working towards a common goal. The activities of these organizations may be aimed solely towards satisfying the needs and interests of their own members or may be led by a desire to help others or to forward a particular common (public) interest. As the negative within the name suggests, a general characteristic of non-profit organizations is that they are institutionalized mediators of citizens which are led by motives other than profit. A legal framework governs the functioning of non-profit organizations.

The civic sector could not exist if individuals were driven purely by self-centered desires. The characteristic that gives birth to these institutions and on which they thrive is altruism, which makes people capable of helping others and the environment without demanding anything in return. Their existence shows us that humans are social creatures who need and seek the presence of others, and are able and prepared to agree and cooperate with others. Fromm and many other psychologists and sociologists have adopted this model of human beings in their work. The social teaching of the Catholic Church is also conceived on this basis. This model of human beings—who in their behavior pursue not only their self-interest, but also that of the collective in which and with which they live—is embraced by Etzioni (1995) and others.

3. Comparing the Public and Private Sectors

In an effort to clarify the characteristics and connections of the three regulators dealt with in the previous section, a brief discussion of the differences between the public and private sectors would be worthwhile. It is a given in respect of the private sector that the individuals and organizations within it make decisions for themselves, led by their own self-interest. Decisions in the public sector, on the other hand, are influenced by many individuals and institutions, and the main objective in the decision-making process is the formulation and promotion of the public interest. The public sector may be compared to a large household which accumulates resources through the efforts of its members; within the household, decisions are made about how the resources will be used.

Government inhabits the public sector, while 'for-profit' organizations reside in the private sector. Non-profit organizations may be understood to be part of a special sector which lies between the public and private sectors: the civic sector (see Table 1.5, 'Domain of the Civic Sector').

It is generally accepted that public institutions contribute to the general good. Public institutions, if they function well, are without doubt as important to societal development as economic resources. The difficulty lies in the fact that it is not always clear what the public interest may be, nor how public institutions should be composed or function such that they operate effectively from an administrative or managerial viewpoint.

Public policy aims to satisfy the public interest in that it deals with social problems which cannot be solved by individuals. It functions in the public interest even though it cannot do everything for everyone. Defining the public interest is often an issue in the course of social and political negotiations and is sometimes the cause of conflict.

This raises the question of whether criteria exist with which the difference between the public and private sectors may be clarified. One option is to define the public sector as that which is financed by the public budget, or possibly from para-fiscal sources such as social security funds. This criterion is insufficient, however, in that it overlooks the regulatory role of legislation. The public sector may also be identified by the government's political and legislative activities and their consequences, or even by what the government does to benefit its citizens, such as provide financial assistance, services, and employment, and even engage in manufacturing. This explanation, however, would reduce the public sector to government administration and would eliminate public self-government. Lane (1993) proposes six fundamental criteria which may be used in the search for the answer to this question (Table 1.3).

Table 1.3 Criteria Distinguishing the Public and Private Sectors

Criterion	Sector	
	Public sector	Private sector
Political power	Government power	Individual freedom
Consumption and investment	Public consumption and investment	Private consumption and investment
Characteristics of decision-making	Political or administrative decision-making	Private decision-making
Provision of goods, benefits, and services	Public goods, benefits, and services	Private goods, benefits, and services
Ownership	Public ownership	Private ownership
Employment	Public sector	Private sector

Turning to the individual criteria included in the table we may formulate a series of questions related to the various methods of drawing lines of demarcation between the public and private sectors:

i. What is the proper place of government power in society; in other words, how comprehensive should individual freedom be? (Problem of freedom.)

ii. What portion of the total resources created by society should be utilized by the government in terms of public consumption and investment? (Problem of allocation.)

iii. How large should the government budget be? In other words, how much individual income should be created without government intervention? (Problem of distribution.)

iv. What portion of goods and services provided by the government should be produced by the government? (Problem of production.)

v. How much production capacity should be owned by the state? (Problem of ownership.)

vi. What portion of the workforce should be employed in the public sector? (Problem of employment.)

A fundamental problem of the market is that not everyone who would like to or who could participate in it is able to do so. On the other hand, the market makes possible an uncountable amount of individual decisions (choices) in a form which maximizes the total wealth of society. The effectiveness of the market, of course, depends on its structure and institutional orderliness. (This will be discussed in detail in chapter 2.)

One fundamental problem of administration is that citizens' preferences rule in the public sector only if an institution exists which discovers them, expresses them, and declares them to be legitimate. On the other hand, the administration may provide subsistence to all, especially to those who do not have an opportunity to (or who could not) make a livelihood in the market.

Okun (1975) postulates that as the relative contribution of extra-market distribution increases the total expendable wealth of society can be expected to diminish. He makes a comparison with a leaky bucket: if only a small quantity of water is carried, we lose little; the more water we try to carry, the more we lose.

The domain of the public and private sectors may be defined on the micro- or macro-level. On the micro-level every good or service is judged on the basis of whether it should be allocated through the market or through the public administration, taking into consideration the applicability of chosen criteria—for example, efficiency or equity. On the macro-level it is possible to bind the development of the public sector to economic growth, so as not to disrupt the balance of both sectors. However, Wildavsky (1980) warns that the public sector may expand if the economy is growing, but in a period of economic stagnation or decline it is not always feasible to limit the public sector, except in cases of national distress.

The public sector is the antithesis of the private sector, where individuals or firms decide for themselves in accordance with their private interests. In the public sphere many individuals and institutions participate in and are influenced

Table 1.4 Comparison of the Characteristics of a Public Institution with Those of a Private Enterprise

Characteristic	Type of institution	
	Public institution	Private firm
Who decides	Parliament and Government	Owner(s)/ Management
Interest	Public interest/ Group interests	Private interests
Probability of dissolution	Low	Higher
Form of regulation	Law, administration, Budgetary limitations	Performance in the market
Motivation	Responsibility/ personal Gain of civil servants	Profit
Nature of implementation	Inter-institutional, Sometimes inter-branch	Dependent on the firm
Organizational structure	More formalized	Less restrictive
Nature of aims	Many aims of a qualitative nature	Maximizing profit in a quantifiable way
Conflicts among aims	Frequent	Rarely
Possibility of measuring aims	Low	High
Legal regulation	High	Lower
Evaluation of results	Election, expertise, legal procedure	Cost-benefit analysis
Openness of procedures and availability of information	Higher	Lower
Rules governing internal operation	Established in detail in the form of binding norms	More general
Inclination towards innovation	Lower	Higher
Tension between administrators, managers, and specialists	Higher	Lower
Centralization	Higher	Lower
Mutual dependency of various organizations	Higher	Lower
Main controlling parameters	Maintaining procedures	Effects of their activities
Sensitivity to clients' needs	Lower	High
Possibility of clients refusing goods*	Low, only by means of elections	High, no binding contracts
Predominating views of managers	Long-term	Short-term
Job security	Higher	Lower
Management style	Routine	Entrepreneurial
Sensitivity to the abilities of the leadership	Higher	Lower
Primary source of income	Public budget	Payments of customers

Source: Lane (1993) with additions and modifications.

* "Exit" (refusing to close a contract in the market) is judged by Hirschman (1970), Kornai (1990), Mannheim (1991), Ringen (1987) and others as a more effective method of refusing goods and services than voting (in elections).

by decision-making. The public sphere is where the public interest is formulated and supported—in the production and distribution of public goods, among other things. Public goods may not be designated to particular owners, nor may people be divided into those who pay for their consumption and those who do not.

In addition to the general characteristics of both sectors, the typical attributes of institutions of one or the other type may be analyzed and compared: a public institution in contrast to a private firm (Table 1.4). Of course, this provides only a general overview of their basic features and tendencies.

4. A Marginalized Sector

In our consideration of the public and private sectors so far we have discussed government and the market. The civic sector is in many ways inextricably interlinked with both (Table 1.5).

Table 1.5 Domain of the Civic Sector

Sector	Public sector	Private sector
Allocation mechanism Criterion of activity	Public budget	Market
Public interest	Government	Civic sector
Profit	—	For-profit sector

While government depends on political processes and manages its affairs by means of legislation and public budgets, the private sector uses the market to optimize decisions about production and the exchange of goods. The civic sector, on the other hand, needs reliable information about human needs if it is to satisfy them in areas where they are not being adequately satisfied by either the for-profit sector or the government. The civic sector is independent of the government; in this sense, it is part of the private sector. Its activities are not motivated by profit, however, but by the desire to satisfy the interests of a specific community; in this sense, it is part of the public sector. For this reason a number of authors recommend that the civic sector be treated as a distinct third sector in which non-profit organizations abide by rules different from the laws of the market and from the functioning of government and its institutions.

> There is also a third sector which, by combining particular features of intervention with others of a free market, may . . . avoid the failures of the two poles and be preferable to either extreme. Hybrid institutions that encourage initiative and enterprise, and are subject to covering their costs, but are at the same time accountable to the public, can harness the best of both sectors . . . The strength of civil society and of non-profit organizations in particular often lies not in opposing the public sector, but in cooperating with it, whether for finance, or for replication of successful

ventures, or for support in opposing exploitative local power elites. In other circumstances, for example when faced with a predatory state, their function is to combat it. (Streeten, 1993)

Analysts of civic-sector development call attention to the fact that non-profit organizations tend to form where neither the market nor government are effective. It may perhaps be legitimate to conceive the *raison d'être* of non-profit organizations as providing a sort of 'bypass' in relation to the market and government, although such a definition does not fully capture their role. In the long run, non-profit organizations cannot replace the market or government in their primary functions. In many cases, however, non-profit organizations are able to complement them.

The following chapters of section 1 are dedicated to more detailed explanation of each regulator. We will also return to the weighty theme of searching for a dynamic balance between these regulators.

2. The Market

The market resembles fire: it is a good servant, but a cruel master.

1. Introduction

This chapter proposes a general definition of the market as a regulator of human activity. We will analyze the strengths and shortcomings of the market and, in conclusion, look at several recent examples which illustrate how complicated and ambivalent market principles can be when considered the 'conquerors' of sectors which were previously regulated by the government.

Since 1989 a number of significant social changes have guaranteed a renaissance in the role of the market. The historical attempt to substitute the market with central planning—a directive method of steering the economy—failed in every respect. The shortcomings of the inefficient, supply-driven economy had a negative impact on people's lives, as a result of which a clear majority of citizens put their hopes in a renewed market economy. Many positive changes happened relatively quickly: there was a rapid development of private sector business and services, a wide selection of earlier inaccessible goods became available, and city centers were renovated and reconstructed. It became clear relatively soon, however, that both the politicians' and the public's expectations concerning the introduction of the market economy had been exaggerated in many instances. In the post-revolution euphoria few people realized that the market was not all-encompassing; that it was not good always and for everything; that it was only an instrument which could be inappropriately used or even abused.

From a political science standpoint the exchange of goods in the market is governed by specific forms of regulation, behavioral control, and cooperation. From an economic standpoint it is irrefutable that supply and demand, profit and loss, allocate scarce resources (while respecting given restrictions) more efficiently than any alternative regulatory mechanism (Barry, 1987). The market is therefore the best engine, instigator, and motivator of economic growth.

It has already been established that the functioning of the market is based on voluntary exchange agreements between buyer and seller. The ideal model of a market economy is balanced. In the uncomplicated world of the market and within a perfectly competitive environment price levels evolve such that no other combination of inputs and outputs exists which would increase the profit of one or more participants in the market exchange without decreasing someone else's profit. This maximizes the potential attainable wealth of society. At the same time, the prices of inputs and outputs of production and consumption are such that the supply of all goods is equal to the demand for them. Economists refer to this as Pareto-efficient distribution.

This distribution, however, bears no relation to the distribution of wealth among individual actors. In other words, it does not reflect total wealth distribution among the members of a given society. Were the market given free reign, the circular and cumulative processes brought about by supply and demand would make those who already have a large amount of resources at their disposal even wealthier, and the poor would lose even the modest amount with which they entered the market (Myrdal, 1968). This trait of the free market is sometimes called its 'centrifugal effect': the poor are flung to the periphery while the wealthy congregate around the center. In support of this theory Barry (1987) observes that unemployment and overconsumption are effects caused by the long-term functioning of a free market unchecked by outside regulators.

It is now time to analyze the strengths and shortcomings of the market as a regulator of social interactions in greater detail.

2. Market Strengths

"The market . . . is a general system of horizontal relationships between free and equal individuals. It is an arena in which people freely choose, where they enter into voluntary contracts with each other, and, thanks to this, realize their wishes, desires, needs, and preferences" (Klaus, 1996, 304). The market provides a tremendous amount of information about what people wish to gain and what is offered to them, and, by means of prices, coordinates the supply of these goods and their demand among a great number of actors.

In comparison with government, the market is advantageous in that it: (i) is able to maximize economic efficiency; (ii) tends to innovate; (iii) adjusts rapidly to changing conditions; (iv) replicates successful experiments; (v) abandons obsolete activities; (vi) performs complex tasks effectively; and (vii) creates opportunities for the productive use of human invention and enterprise.

3. Market Shortcomings

If no criterion other than the maximization of global economic efficiency were applied and an ideal market environment existed, it would be sensible to aspire to Pareto-efficiency and give free reign to the market. However, in politics economic efficiency is not the only important criterion, and economic reality never entirely reflects the ideal of a purely competitive market.

3.1 Failures of the Market in Applying Criteria Other than Economic Efficiency

Let us now consider five criteria taken from various normative models of society.

3.1.1 Minimizing Inequalities in the Distribution of Goods

Two considerations may be adduced in support of this criterion:

i. If we suppose that marginal utility decreases as wealth increases, the same unit of wealth would satisfy poorer people more. If this is the case, greater equality in the distribution of goods leads to a higher total social yield. To the Czechs this is a decidedly sensitive issue because they lost the greater part of their aristocracy during and after the Thirty Years War in the first half of the 1600s. People of Czech nationality—revived in the eighteenth and nineteenth centuries—generally remained in the lower and middle classes.

ii. In a democratic society, in which support for the political regime and the will of the people are expressed in elections, it is necessary to cultivate the voluntary agreement of a majority of citizens in respect of government policies. Wide social differences can threaten the fundamental legitimacy of a country's economic and political regime. The balance inherent in this relationship is explained by Dahrendorf (1985), who refers to the unwritten social contract in terms of which the government agrees to uphold particular fundamental norms, even if maintaining them requires the use of violence. One aspect of the social contract is the rule of law as the basic instrument regulating social relationships, but this is only one half of the contract. The second half is the acceptance of the welfare state (public social services) as an integrated component of modern government.

Let us consider this problem at a deeper level. Okun (1975) assumes that we are seeking a solution which would ensure both economic efficiency and just distribution (dividing goods such that a certain portion of their consumption is guaranteed to each person). We know that Pareto-efficiency is attained if economic efficiency is maximized, but that does not address the issue of just distribution. This solution is based exclusively on market principles. It is possible to imagine a completely different situation in which everyone received the same amount (maximally just distribution), but economic efficiency would be zero. This situation would be possible only if the government had absolute power and the market were not allowed to function at all. Virtually every government in the world (excluding such excesses as the Khmer Rouge) works to sweeten the regulation of the market and government such that an optimal balance between economic efficiency and just distribution is achieved. Nonetheless, it is not always the case that as distribution becomes more just, economic efficiency decreases.

It is ironic that a feasible, technologically enlightened combination of the market and government can be attained with the maximum possible economic efficiency, maintaining at the same time the established conditions of just distribution. Economic efficiency of this kind would never be as complete as Pareto-efficiency, but it would be ethically, socially, and (under democratic conditions) politically acceptable. The key mistake of all socialist governments was their attempt to substitute the government for the market even in places where the latter was essential. The resulting economic efficiency was substantially below the minimum necessary to attain the government's goal of just distribution. In this respect, socialist governments dug their own graves: their legitimacy evaporated not because they distributed goods unjustly, but because their economies collapsed. It is not necessary to mention that the opposite extreme is also dangerous—when economic efficiency is strengthened even at the cost of extremely unjust distribution. The legitimacy of a regime promoting this 'primitive' form of capitalism is undermined because it completely neglects the criterion of just distribution. This leads to the problem of how concretely to optimize the regulatory power of the market and government in relation to the ultimate goals of society. The present book is largely an attempt to address this issue.

3.1.2 Preserving Institutional Value
To understand this criterion, let us consider the family as an institution traditionally protected by the Church or conservative political philosophy. One of its intrinsic values is to protect its dependent members. Prostitution, the offer of sexual services on the market for pay, is seen by the Church and conservative political philosophy as a threat to the family unit and morality, and for that reason it is forbidden or severely limited.

3.1.3 Human Dignity
In order to enter the market a person must be able to offer something for exchange. Someone who has little or nothing to offer is not able to enter the market or has extremely limited possibilities. Because survival depends on consuming at least a minimum amount of private goods, allocating them efficiently on the market could seriously harm individuals who have limited access to it, leading to their deprivation or early demise. Extreme examples are people who are pushed by the market to the periphery of society, such as beggars and the homeless, but also single mothers, children of impoverished parents, and the mentally or physically handicapped.

3.1.4 Cultivating and Fulfilling Human Potential
Advocates of this criterion presume that inequality in respect of the basic conditions of individual development, where only the market could change the situation, is unjust (Potůček, 1991; 1992). Human beings should be given equal opportunities to develop and realize their potential. Even economic analyses of the prosperity of contemporary societies always focus on how to increase the quality of human resources, of human capital. This illustrates the fact that the market is not capable of meeting particular criteria—for example, in respect of education, health care, or the full-blooded participation of individuals in the life of society.

3.1.5 A Sustainable Way of Life

This criterion goes beyond the framework of considerations of what is good for individuals and society. It considers the consequences of our actions for other living beings and the environment. This criterion does not mesh with a predatory relationship to other people or different ways of life, or exploiting the environment, which are often the products of market-oriented efforts to maximize profit (Vavroušek, 1993).

Up to this point we have examined failures of the market which result from applying criteria other than economic efficiency. Now we shall investigate failures—to which Arrow first brought attention at the end of the 1960s—which are caused by a market environment which does not correspond with the ideal model of a market economy.

3.2 Market Shortcomings Caused by the Absence of an Ideal Market Environment

3.2.1 The Existence of Public Goods

Private goods are defined in terms of the rivalry of consumption (something that is consumed by one cannot be consumed by another) and the absolute ability to exclude others from ownership and use (an individual is the exclusive owner or user of a given good). The ability to exclude from ownership or use has two aspects: physical and legal. The legal aspect is referred to as the execution of ownership rights. Public goods are, by contrast, characteristically non-exclusive and/or non-transferable to a specific owner or user. Therefore they cannot be optimally allocated by means of the market. Examples of public goods are a country's cultural heritage, national defense, and territorial integrity. (Note: The border between public and private goods is not established once and for all; it changes and evolves under the influence of the development of technology, the development of social institutions, human values—ethical principles accepted by the population—and political decisions [Mishan, 1981]).

3.2.2 The Existence of Externalities

An externality is defined as any negative or positive consequence (cost or benefit) resulting from a market contract (whether it concerns production or consumption) which is transferred to someone not involved with the relevant market relationship.

3.2.3 A Natural Monopoly in Respect of Supply or Demand

A monopoly on the part of a supplier occurs when fixed production costs are high in comparison to variable costs, such that the average price decreases with an increase in demand. Provided these conditions are fulfilled, one firm is able to produce the given good for a lower price than anyone else on the market. A market relationship characterized by a single buyer (monopsonist) may also exist.

3.2.4 Informational Asymmetry between Seller and Buyer

Informational asymmetry between seller and buyer occurs when the quality of goods to be purchased becomes apparent only during or after consumption.

We can distinguish between three types of goods—those whose quality: (i) is known before consumption (the majority of consumer goods); (ii) becomes apparent only during consumption (most services); and (iii) becomes evident only after consumption (most medical services).

With the second and—particularly—the third types of goods, the danger exists that the seller will misuse an informational advantage to obtain an unwarranted profit.

3.2.5 The Changing Preferences of Market Contractors

The ideal model of market economics assumes that participants have stable preferences which are expressed by the relationship of their consumption capacity to the supposed gain. Clearly, however, preferences can be influenced by an external agent in many circumstances—for example, governments often launch publicity campaigns to prevent drug abuse or promote healthier diets. Such changes are motivated mainly by the desire to remove potential negative externalities of human behavior.

3.2.6 Neglecting the Future

The market reacts only to immediate interests; it is myopic and can encourage the maximization of short-term profits, even if that leads to long-term losses. Manufacturers aim for rapid returns on their invested capital; the possible long-term consequences for people of production or consumption are often not taken into consideration.

Besides the previously mentioned failures, many other possible negative consequences of the market have been discussed in the literature. The downsides of its adaptability—including market insecurity and instability—may lead to negative social and economic effects such as mass layoffs, bankruptcies, and economic and ecological crises.

Example:

After 1989 the government of the young Czechoslovak democracy decided to move out of weapons production. This decision had the greatest impact on the large weapons production factories that were built in Slovakia during socialism, which up to that point had provided weapons systems to many former Soviet bloc countries. This was the only or the main industrial activity in towns such as Martin and Dubnica nad Váhom. Commuting to work from valley to valley in mountainous central Slovakia is difficult. The scaling down of these mammoth enterprises caused extremely high local unemployment.

4. The Market in the Czech Republic after 1989

The renaissance of the market as a regulator of human activity, the bearer of economic prosperity, and the ally of a democratic political order was given the green light after 1989. The introduction of the market economy had many positive effects on people's lives. No one could realistically expect that such a fundamental change in living conditions would not have negative effects as well. Moreover, many processes related to the introduction of a market economy and changes in ownership (restitution, privatization, decentralization to regions and municipalities of previous state ownership) were not sufficiently prepared from the administrative and legal points of view. They were poorly conceived by the politicians and the public, who inadequately and unrealistically predicted the consequences for society of realizing a free market.

The form of individual public policies always depends on the general political climate and the 'choice of society'. Between 1989 and the 1992 elections an attempt was made to implement the regulatory powers of government and the market in a balanced way, whereas after the 1992 elections particular emphasis was placed on the market. Between 1990 and 1992 the Czechoslovak government consisted of a broad coalition of liberal and social-democratic orientation. Since 1992 a rightist coalition of conservative and neo-liberal orientation has been in power, led by Prime Minister Václav Klaus. A dogmatic and unhealthy preference for the market has been visible, especially in areas in which the government has traditionally played a primary role, the public interest being manifested and executed there to a greater degree than elsewhere (Gabal, 1996). This becomes evident in the following examples, taken from the spheres of law enforcement and housing. (Similar results in respect of organized crime are analyzed in more detail in chapter 10, 'Corruption and the Mafia', while health care is examined in chapter 8, 'Privatization'. These themes are also addressed in chapter 7, 'Seeking a Balance', which discusses the balance between government, market, and civic sector.)

Law and Order Policy

Between 1989 and 1993 the number of recorded criminal acts in the Czech Republic nearly tripled. The number of investigations undertaken within the same period quadrupled. At the same time, the percentage of crimes solved dropped sharply. A significant majority were crimes against property, mainly robberies. The profit motive was most visible in fraud, pandering, production of unauthorized drugs, blackmail, extortion, abuse of power by public officials, and corruption (Cejp, 1995).

These developments are clearly the result of suddenly obtained political and economic freedoms—along with a new openness in society—combined with a low level of trust and legitimacy, and a lack of power in the hands of the repressive organs of the state (the police and the courts). The regulation of the market was loosened at the same time as the repressive organs of the government were weakened. "New patterns and criteria of social success founded on one's position in the market are being created" (Cejp, 1995, 14).

"Purely for business reasons, private security agencies are not interested in increasing general safety and legality because the sources of their prosperity are not legality and ensuring the safety of citizens, but exactly the opposite. Security agencies' economic dependency on developing criminality and operation on its fringes can lead to a conflict of interest" (Gabal, 1994, 93).

Insufficient regulation of private security agencies has led to their frequent involvement in criminal activities. "The government has made room for commercially guaranteed security, the market for safety, rather than safety guaranteed on the principle of citizens' rights and the rule of law. This will result in the probable expansion of criminality. As a result, safety is guaranteed with less effectiveness than could be achieved by government ... The goal of law and order policy should not be to increase the privatization or commercialization of security, but rather to limit and repress it to a minimum" (Gabal, 1994, 95).

In a situation in which the government neglects to care for the security of citizens, citizens begin to take their own initiatives. Security which depends on the individual does not produce legality, but rather subjective, personal, and private conceptions of justice.

"There is a rising number of crimes linked with debt collection, property, obligations,   · and contracts. This is evidence of a decreasing belief in justice, equality and the rule of law, and conversely an increasing 'addiction' to secure justice and rights through personal initiative and pressure activities. In a freer environment of unserviceable or non-functioning justice and an ineffective guarantee by the government of personal safety and rights, the private commercial sphere of business and safety—the law enforcement and justice business—quickly moves in ... When governmental effectiveness in this sphere is visibly problematic and worsening, securing the safety of citizens is not a 'premium' service, but rather a necessity for a certain stratum of the population. Safety becomes a question of wealth and the willingness to pay; it stops being a universal right of citizens and becomes a privilege, depending on the level of wealth ... There are two alternatives. One is to continue to take responsibility from government and put it in the hands of citizens and private initiatives. Another is for government to take responsibility and limit market-based dealings in safety to a clearly defined area, beyond the elementary functioning of civil society." (Gabal, 1994, 93n)

Housing Policy
The housing policy recommendations of 1990 emphasized the government's essential role in creating adequate economic, legislative, social, and organizational conditions. Proposals from 1991 and 1992 pay much less attention to this issue. A proposal from 1991 instead stresses the removal of barriers which could discourage the spontaneous development of housing units by the market, while by 1992 the situation is beginning to be portrayed more realistically. In the course of 1991 and 1992 Czech housing policy came to view the housing market—in contrast with 1990—not as a means to an end, but as an end in itself (Valentová, 1995, 14n). None of the market instruments gradually introduced by the Klaus government into housing policy between 1992 and 1996 (such as loans and mortgages to build houses and apartments) were able to reverse the decline in new housing construction. Why? Government removed the housing subsidies utilized by the previous regime and did not replace them with new methods soon enough.

A government's inadequate response to the regulatory effects of the market may become visible not only in the direct neglect of particular branches, but also in increased earnings differentials between the private sector (where salaries are dependent on the market position of a given profession) and the public sector (where salaries are based primarily on administrative regulations such as wage tariffs for public servants). Significantly higher—and more rapidly growing—salaries in the private sector have led to a substantial brain drain from the public sector since 1989. Public administration has not responded adequately to the danger caused by this loss of knowledge and expertise. The worst affected branches are education, science, research, and health care. But not only these: "Compared with private means, profit and salaries in private security agencies drain the service ranks, the value of loyalty to citizens, and the value of the law in the police force" (Gabal, 1994, 94).

3. Government

> It is certain that the institutional structure of society is the key variable which encourages and underpins the adaptability, ability, and willingness of society to experiment, search, creatively enterprise, undergo inevitable risks, and learn from its mistakes.
>
> *Lubomír Mlčoch*

1. Introduction

This chapter returns to the definition of government as a regulator of human activities. We will examine its strengths and shortcomings (both generally and in the course of describing particular situations in the Czech Republic since 1989) and, in conclusion, sum up the challenges created by the current state of social development of government and public administration in both the East and the West.

The role and position of government in regulating human activities is an extremely controversial topic because it encompasses conflicting political conceptions and visions. While anarchists are enemies of government by definition, neo-liberals would like to limit its functions to ensuring the safety of free citizens and maintaining the legal order. Institutionalists believe that the vital, multifaceted function of government is to determine the course of society and the economy. Protagonists of collectivist and totalitarian doctrines consider government to be the most important regulator of human activities, representing the interests of society first and foremost, above the interests of individuals. While many ideological positions have been taken on this topic, attempts to apply them in a functioning, modern society leave no doubt that governments exist, that they are developing, that they influence people's lives, and that they are important instruments of regulation.

Example:
Government has traditionally been involved in education. Theoreticians attempt to justify this by pointing out that it is not profitable for entrepreneurs constantly to dedicate their energies to preparing people to be new members of the work force; therefore, in capitalist economies government should pay for education. They argue further that government influence on the content and form of socializing future citizens is an effective way of promoting social cohesion. In addition, government may try to ensure equality of opportunity by means of the national educational system (Kalous, 1996, 86–87).

Political power as a means of regulation, in contrast to other forms such as market forces or indoctrination, is relatively simple. Regulation by the market always requires the sacrifice of something in exchange for the desired gain, and regulation through indoctrination requires time and systematic effort. Governmental control need not be costly, provided that it draws support from an established political power base. However, establishing and maintaining power is costly in itself (in terms of expenses related to maintaining the government apparatus, including repressive elements), and in democratic systems it is complicated—and sometimes expensive—for a given political order to maintain a sufficient degree of legitimacy in the eyes of the public.

Control by means of political power is wielded in two primary ways: (i) by establishing laws which must be obeyed and (ii) by creating legislative or economic conditions that stimulate, repress or directly enforce particular forms of behavior.

The effectiveness of political power as a means of control explains its central position in government. This power is delegated to diverse units of government, which involves itself in market transactions by defining contract conditions and ensuring their fulfillment, and sometimes engages in exchanges itself. The risks of government use of political power as a regulatory device become visible when power is abused or when the original authority vested in government is exceeded.

The basic principles of the functioning of government (public administration) are delineated in the classic theoretical tradition which views government as an instrument for promoting the public good. These principles are described by Plato, Hegel, Weber, Tinbergen, and others.

Another type of model for analyzing public administration is defined by Buchanan, Olson, and others who represent a critical reaction to the classic model. This second model is inspired mainly by public choice theory. The theoretical conception of public choice is often associated with James Buchanan, who views government above all as an institution that represents the interests of various pressure groups (while simultaneously posing as a neutral party which represents the interests of all). Advocates of this theory include former Czech Prime Minister Václav Klaus, who views government as a slave to interest groups. From his standpoint, the establishment of government as guarantor of the public interest is an overly ambitious, even unobtainable, goal because declared public interests are merely facades that conceal real, particular interest groups (1996, especially 261 and 277).

Obviously, these two camps differ considerably in respect of their theoretical conceptions of the role and function—or dysfunction—of government. Basically, these contradictory theories are defined by opposite factors—classic theory by positive assumptions and public choice theory by negative ideas as to the principles of government functioning.

2. Ten Characteristics of the Functioning of Government Incorporating Its Role as Guardian of the Public Interest

(i) The government is an institution which seeks unswervingly to satisfy the public interest.

(ii) The government is a well-informed and competent institution.

(iii) Public servants fulfill their obligations and responsibilities while carrying out their activities in the public sector and, because they are working for the public good, do not abuse their positions for private purposes.

(iv) The duties of public institutions are determined by politicians; nevertheless, they are carried out by non-partisan civil servants whose behavior is based on a model of rational conduct.

(v) Public administration is based on written documentation; bureaucracy is the heart of modern government.

(vi) Public affairs are conducted and resolved in accordance with accepted procedural norms.

(vii) Regulations followed by public administration may be of a technical or legal character. In both cases, they are implemented by capable professional functionaries.

(viii) Tasks or functions are divided into functional subsystems which allow access to authority and the application of sanctions.

(ix) Centralization is functional. Civil servants and their duties are hierarchically ordered, with specified mechanisms for controls and complaints.

(x) Public resources are invested only where necessary to satisfy the public interest.

3. Ten Characteristics of the Functioning of Government When Conceived as a Means of Promoting Private Interests

(i) The government utilizes its political power to gain wealth from private individuals.

(ii) The government is used to forward the self-serving individual or group interests of politicians and civil servants.

(iii) Politicians utilize their position to maximize their personal share of political power.

(iv) Civil servants do not have altruistic motives; their goal is to maximize their own income, prestige, and power by means of public service.

(v) Individuals and organized interest groups take advantage of political influence in order to obtain as large a share as possible of public resources.

(vi) The government does not act according to models of rational conduct, but rather according to models of limited rationality.

(vii) The distinction between politics (the process of making decisions) and administration (the process of applying decisions in accordance with accepted norms) is insignificant.

(viii) The government's functioning is directed not by accepted rules, but by defined political aims.

(ix) It is not realistic to expect that projects prioritized at the top of the hierarchy will be carried out.

(x) Public resources are invested where self-serving individuals or group interests are strongest.

The actual behavior of government and its authorities, of course, corresponds neither to the first nor to the second of these models, but to aspects of both. "Government maximizes neither the public good nor the satisfaction of selfish interests. It attempts to make compromises, to satisfactorily resolve conflict, and to mediate negotiations between individual interest groups. Sometimes it promotes generally beneficial political projects or innovations" (Streeten, 1993, 1290).

The degree to which government is able to prevent particular group and individual interests from superseding the public interest differs from case to case. Democracies have substantial, though never absolute, advantages over totalitarian regimes in this respect. Although abuses exist in all regimes, democracies are best equipped to expose and punish them because power and administration are not controlled solely by formal mechanisms, but also by cultivated and conscious citizens—as well as the civic sector—who can resist government power if the need arises.

At this point in the argument it is worth examining in more detail the strengths and shortcomings of government as a regulator of the activities of people and institutions.

4. Government Strengths

Compared to the market, government authorities are more effective at: policy management; administrative regulation; rapidly mobilizing and utilizing resources; guaranteeing the continuity and stability of services; preventing exploitation and discrimination; ensuring public safety; promoting equality; and maintaining social cohesion and peace.

Decentralized authority and responsibility can have many advantages—or strengths—which are the mirror images of the disadvantages—or shortcomings—of highly centralized systems of government. A general advantage of decentralization is that decision-making is closer to citizens, which allows more feedback. In contrast to centralized systems, a decentralized public administration is better able to adapt to concrete conditions and the wishes of its citizens; it allows more room for experimentation and alternative methods of problem-solving.

5. Government Shortcomings

Theories of government shortcomings analyze deficiencies in electoral systems and in the process of aggregating individual preferences: they describe the risk of publicly elected officials becoming estranged from the voters; they attribute problems to bureaucracy, the role of the mass media, and the power of political lobbying to influence political decisions; they warn of the risks posed by the dominance of organized and articulated minority interests over the dispersed and rarely asserted interests of the majority (and vice-versa); and they investigate the limitations of implementing collective decisions in decentralized systems of government. Many theoretical models and empirical analyses of government shortcomings have emerged from the fields of organizational sociology, institutional economics, public choice theory, public administration, and public policy. However, thus far no one has tried to synthesize these findings into a complete theoretical system similar to the one which addresses market failures.

If we consider the broad meaning of the term 'public administration', including all the processes that contribute to the generation and use of political power (Weimer and Vining, 1992), government shortcomings may be associated with five systems in which they occur: totalitarian regimes, direct democracies, representative democracies, decentralized systems, and the activity of governing itself.

5.1 Shortcomings of Totalitarian Political Systems

5.1.1 Insufficient Internal Regulation
The absence of feedback in totalitarian systems makes them unable to identify adequately changes in external conditions and budding internal problems. Because of this they react inadequately or belatedly, if at all. The absence of feedback is problematic in the political system as well as in the centrally planned economy (Kameníček and Kouba, 1992).

5.1.2 Suppressing Human Creative Potential
In totalitarian systems, people are unable to develop their capabilities and skills sufficiently, which undermines the overall functioning and effectiveness of these systems and results in a frustrated population.

5.2 Failures of Direct Democracy

5.2.1 The Problem with Referendums
In a referendum the very form of the question can influence the outcome of the vote (for example, if the question is posed in the negative as rejection or in the positive as acceptance). It is difficult to formulate a question which is clear yet which includes all of the important issues pertaining to a decision. The specific implementation of a general decision based on the results of a referendum can significantly differ from the true wishes of the majority of voters.

5.2.2 Inexpressive Majority Defeats an Outspoken Minority
When a small group takes a principled and specific stance on a particular issue and the majority takes the opposite stance, the choice of the majority prevails although it may be half-hearted and not representative of their specific interests.

5.3 Failures of Representative Democracy

5.3.1 The Paradox of Voting
The paradox of voting was first described by Condorcet, then by Caroll, and formalized by Arrow (1971). Those who set the conditions in which elections are held have the opportunity to influence the election results and the success of individual candidates.

Example:
Just a few months prior to the 1998 elections the Slovak government coalition passed a new law which, by changing the rules, seriously undermined the opposition parties' prospects of victory.

On the other hand, those whose opinions would not be heard in other circumstances are able constantly to put forward new agendas for consideration and to create disturbances in the political process which can even cause governmental coalitions to fragment and so lead to a state of political imbalance.

5.3.2 'Packaging' Preferences
Many political issues influence voters' decisions. In an election, candidates may win who do not gain majority approval on a single issue as long as they succeed in satisfying individual groups of voters on the particular issues that most concern them.

5.3.3 The Alienation of Elected Representatives from the Interests of Their Electorate
The 'principal agent' theory describes the relationship between the principal, or supreme holder of power (the voter), and the agent who is delegated the authority to wield power (the elected representative). This theory holds that elected representatives may display opportunistic behavior or behavior that does not necessarily reflect—and can sometimes be in direct opposition to—the wishes of the electorate. Controlling the representative's behavior is not simple—it requires time and money and can never be completely effective.

5.3.4 The Influence of Organized Interests (Lobbying)
Policies which provide little benefit to the general public are generally not actively supported because the cost of political activism directed towards the implementation of such policies is greater than the expected benefit. On the other hand, the interests of a small, organized group have a chance of being adopted through active lobbying. Although the policy benefits only that group, its costs are dis-

persed throughout society. Lindblom (1977) points out that this phenomenon unfairly benefits organized economic interests in democratic political systems. This theme is dealt with in more detail in chapter 9.

5.3.5 Restricted Time-Frame
The decision-making time frame for politicians is basically restricted to their current term of office. This means that government, like the market, can be myopic. In other words, the promise of short-term profit can outweigh long-term loss during the decision-making process. One interesting aspect of this fact of democracy is the situation of unborn citizens, children, and youths, who do not have the right to vote, although their lives may be influenced by current decisions.

5.3.6 Influence of the Mass Media
The role of the mass media in shaping public opinion has been clearly recognized and systematically analyzed in the literature. The presentation and content of information have an impact on the public's perception of public affairs. This does not have to involve purposeful manipulation—editors' or journalists' choice of genres, agendas, and events, as well as their targeting of particular types of viewers, listeners, or readers, is sufficient. As Weimer and Vining (1992) put it: "The political system, for the most part, makes it impossible to base public policy on responsible consideration of social costs and benefits."

5.4 Typical Failures in the Functioning of Public Administration

5.4.1 Inefficiency and Inflexibility of Bureaucracies
This failure of public administration may be explained in terms of several mutually supporting conditions: (i) There are inherent difficulties in evaluating benefits, especially those deriving from government activity. Exact criteria with which to determine which departments function well and which poorly are rarely available. (However, in the last ten years special methods to overcome this handicap have been developed which create routine and objective evaluations of the activities of civil servants. In the United States, for example, a special federal bureau called the General Accounting Office exists to evaluate the benefits deriving from the activities of American government authorities.) (ii) Insufficient competition means there is minimal pressure to respond to the changing needs of citizens and leads to rigidity in the structure of services rendered. (iii) Binding budgetary regulations hinder the ability to respond flexibly to changing conditions.

5.4.2 The Alienation of Government Bureaucracy from Its Purpose
This failure in public administration is caused by the difficulty of ensuring accountability, particularly in the following relationships: politicians and their subordinates; superiors and their subordinates in a bureaucracy; civil servants and citizens. In all of these relationships, alienation is possible because of informational asymmetry, that is, the second subject in the relationship does not possess as much information as the first. Informational superiority may easily be

misused to forward private (individual or group) interests to the detriment of the public interest. Proponents of public choice theory go so far as to assume that maximizing personal benefit is the primary motive of politicians and government officials.

5.5 Shortcomings of Decentralized Systems

5.5.1 The Difficulty of Governing in Decentralized Systems
Decentralized systems entail more complex government, particularly when it is necessary to win the acceptance of and implement decisions that affect numerous decentralized units. Decision-making is delayed and the cost of implementing policies is increased due to the need for negotiation and coordination among the participating actors. Highly autonomous lower levels of administration make the rapid and direct implementation of decisions at a higher level difficult.

5.5.2 The Threat of Group Interests Being Promoted at the Expense of the Public Interest
Decentralization facilitates heterogeneous local and group interests, all of which attempt to 'harness' decentralized units of government for private benefit. This weakens the government's ability to implement comprehensive policies and undermines its primary function as the guarantor of the public interest.

5.5.3 Fiscal Externalities
When authority to determine the composition and extent of public budgets and taxes is significantly decentralized, lower-level decision-makers may tend not to resolve problems. This may negatively impact public budgets at a higher level.

These descriptions of government failures are derived from the analysis of concrete processes. Relevant theories, however, have not been sufficiently discussed to enable us to offer a definitive diagnosis of when, where, and why these failures actually occur.

6. Challenges to Public Administration

Public administration works relatively well if the environment is stable, assignments are relatively simple, and citizens are not overly concerned about the quality of the services they require. The contemporary world, however, does not fit this scenario. Public administration has confronted and continues to face significant changes in its environment: the process of social transformation in Central and Eastern Europe is characterized by many fluid and turbulent changes; the global market is gaining power, which places extreme pressure on economic institutions to be flexible and adaptable; an 'information society' is being born in which citizens have access to relevant information almost as quickly as their leaders; a growing number of highly qualified workers require autonomy in their work; people's needs are becoming more and more diverse.

This context requires extremely effective and adaptable institutions and highly qualified and motivated employees. Traditional bureaucratic institutions, however, do not have the means to attract people of this kind: the distribution of responsibility, subordination, hierarchical structure, and tough controls do not meet their expectations in respect of an advantageous and attractive job. Experience has shown that the effectiveness and attractiveness of professions in public administration may be raised by, for example, delegating particular powers and responsibilities—and of course control—to lower levels.

Even public administration is tackling the prevailing problem of rational choice. With limited intellectual capacity at its disposal, public administration is confronted with the complex problems of modern civilization. Its stereotypical reaction is to divide the problems into small segments, focus specialized skills on each of them, and make standardized decisions by applying solutions which have been developed for various categories of problems. However, government is also faced with problems created by this very approach: shortcomings in coordination, breakdowns in information flow, information overload of decision-makers, institutional failures caused by the opportunistic behavior of administrators, and rapid changes in the circumstances related to the chosen method of resolution. Within the governmental framework conflicting motives arise. Political power is accepted because it brings security, expected rewards, and future benefits to administrators; however, activities which are often unpleasant are also required. The reaction to potential punishment may be unhealthy in that individuals and institutions are taught how to avoid punishment rather than how to accomplish what is necessary (Skinner).

Many of these government failures, though serious, are not fatal. We are not condemned once and for all to have to put up with such imperfect bureaucratic institutions. If Drucker's view (1994) is correct, that life in and with organizations is the destiny of contemporary people, it is important not to adopt an attitude of hopelessness. "We are definitely not witnessing 'the death of government'. On the contrary, we need a confident, strong, and very active government. We must decide between a large but impotent government and a government which is strong because it concentrates on decision-making and influencing, leaving the execution to others. We need a government which knows how to govern and does so. Not a government which 'administers', but a government which truly governs" (Drucker, 1994).

Example:

Osborne and Gaebler (1992) have postulated the 'ten commandments' of modern government administration. They focus on innovation and instruments that government can and should implement in order to cope with present and future requirements: (i) catalytic government: steering rather than rowing; (ii) community-owned government: empowering rather than serving; (iii) competitive government: injecting competition into service delivery; (iv) mission-driven government: transforming rule-driven organizations; (v) results-oriented government: funding outcomes, not inputs; (vi) customer-driven government: meeting the needs of the customer, not the bureaucracy; (vii) enterprising government: earning rather than spending; (viii) anticipatory government: preventing rather than curing; (ix) decentralized government: moving from hierarchy to participation and teamwork; (x) market-oriented government: leveraging change through the market.

Lane (1993) adds that institutions may be adapted so that they better understand people's interests and concerns—and so that the interests of government and its civil servants are not considered more important than those of citizens.

As contemporary government develops, its tendency is to move from traditional forms of direct enforcement towards indirect methods of influencing people's activities. Government is moving away from supplying services directly, leaving more and more to specialized firms, which frees its hands to realize its designated regulatory function.

People react more responsibly if they have control over their own circumstances rather than being undermined by exterior forces. However, a prerequisite for applying a governing strategy based on this human tendency is a legal order which ensures that citizens have a right to information about the activities of public institutions and access to their meetings.

Example:
A fundamental reform of public administration took place in New Zealand in the 1980s in the course of which its obsolete components were removed. The basic reform strategy was to delineate administration in accordance with its basic functions: political management, administration, and service provision. Everything in the original system was separated, in the form of either state-owned for-profit enterprises operating in the market—especially in the sphere of infrastructure—or the privatization of formerly state-owned firms, such as dockyards, banks, and oil companies. Regulations that limited competition in the private sector and, to some extent, in the service providing portion of the public sector, were put aside.

As stated in the conclusion issued by the UN Conference on Public Administration and Development that took place in New York in April 1996, in order to resolve the pressing problems of our time "not less, but better government is needed" (Public Administration, 1996).

7. Developmental Changes in the Czech Government since 1989

It would be presumptuous to attempt to give an exhaustive overview of the strengths and shortcomings of public administration in the Czech Republic since 1989. Nevertheless, several examples that typify the development of the Czech state over this period may provide helpful pointers.

In 1989 government in the Czech Republic was extremely centralized: the higher levels of administration had all-encompassing hierarchical control over the lower levels. At the same time, the Communist Party had more or less absolute power over the system. The result was the merging of the executive and legislative functions of government. The Communist Party stood above the law, and independent internal control of the state apparatus did not exist. Obedience was a fundamental prerequisite of work in the state or party.

The role of government during the transformation was defined by two interrelated, but mutually exclusive needs: (i) to define relatively constant 'rules of the game' and (ii) extensive change and freedom from the burdens of the past. "Reform efforts certainly have to aim towards stability, dependability and continuity in the administrative system. Nevertheless, existing structures and procedures must not inhibit later changes and modifications which will certainly occur in relation to the transformation of internal conditions. Stability, therefore, must be combined with flexibility, dependability with openness, constancy with adaptability" (Hesse, 1993, 250).

Influenced by the neo-liberal doctrine, whose staunchest supporter was former Prime Minister Václav Klaus, an oversimplified view of the need to minimize the role of government was put forward. But at least there was a concept and a vision: in Poland, according to Kolarska-Bobinska (n.d.), the transformation began without a comprehensive plan concerning how the role of government should be changed. However, the concept dangerously underestimated the regulatory role of the government in favor of the market.

On the other hand, some experts came to believe that if the state did not put a stop to its own disintegration, which had been put into motion at the beginning of the societal changes, the transforming countries would find themselves facing a protracted crisis (Hesse, 1993; Manning, 1993). For this reason—and taking into consideration the continuing tendency of citizens to depend on the state—they believed that the transformation could not be successful without strong government intervention.

Where does the truth lie? Certainly we will not find it in unfinished and shallow discussions about how good—or how destructive—it is to have a strong government. Such discussions lead us astray precisely because they are both abstract and extremely simplistic. We cannot seek a government that is simply strong, weak, or nonexistent. Rather we must consider a government with defined goals, structures, and functions, even the instruments it utilizes, and relate them to existing conditions. Sometimes that requires a retreat from former spheres of influence, particularly in reducing the government's role in economic regulation. At other times it means creating new governmental regulatory institutions in areas in which they function well, such as the war against drugs or against organized crime.

Surprisingly, the readiness of the executive branch in the former Czechoslovakia to implement new policies and reforms in 1989 proved to be greater than that of their fellows in Poland or Hungary. Despite the fact that the public administration as a whole was marked by considerable volatility it was capable of action. This, combined with a new government made up of economists, meant that the conditions were ripe for the rapid adoption of economic reforms, including the introduction of an unprecedented voucher privatization scheme.

The initial phases of economic reform, despite all the mistakes and omissions, were successfully managed. This has been confirmed by a number of specialists and experts in international studies, and given additional weight by the positive results of studies conducted to determine public opinion. Although potential problems were delineated in analyses by many economists (including Mertlík, Mlčoch, Klacek, and Sojka), they were initially obscured by the macroeconomic success of Czech economic reforms in the first years of transformation. Some of the most important problems were the unstable and poorly functioning legal and institutional framework for privatization, unclear ownership relationships, and slow and inadequate financial restructuring and modernization. These shortcomings became increasingly evident in and after 1996, after which the Klaus government quickly began to lose public support; at the end of 1997 Klaus had to resign as Prime Minister of the Czech Republic.

Reform in other areas of society was retarded, even at the expense of economic growth. In many cases, the government reacted only when problems became severe; sometimes it did not react at all.

Examples:

1. In 1993 and 1994 the Parliament did nothing to resolve personnel problems in the army and only changed its position when the problems became acute (Sarvaš, 1995, 116).

2. The same can be said about the delayed reaction of the Parliament and government to the unsuccessful health care reforms. "The Ministry of Health was unable to recognize the causes of particular failures within the system of health insurance in time and did not deal with the appropriate competencies of individual actors . . . Its main failure was that it did not develop additional procedural regulations for health insurance or make necessary changes in the current regulations" (Háva and Kružík, 1996, 12).

3. Public administration, particularly the Ministry of the Interior, acted only after a marked delay to solve problems linked with increasing criminality. The police were able to solve less than one-fifth of thefts and burglaries. At the same time, the number of crimes rose, which meant both that citizens were at greater risk and that criminals had a greater statistical probability of escaping unpunished (Gabal, 1994, 85–86).

The causes of these and similar shortcomings may be more easily understood when viewed within the following framework. The government showed insufficient political will to address critical areas of public policy, especially increasing criminality and problems related to education, health care, and housing. Furthermore, the public administration devoted inadequate time, energy, and legislative and intellectual capacity to resolving fundamental questions on the basis of fully analyzed and evaluated alternative conceptions. Not enough relevant analytical information was accumulated within the public administration to create an effective legislative framework and to allocate financial resources such that promising innovations and developments could be supported. The reform of the regional public administration was delayed, causing the protracted temporary division of competencies in many areas (health care, environment, transport, education, and social security) and at the same time expanded particular ministries within the regions. A number of politicians and public servants lacked the moral character necessary to carry out their roles in public administration. There was insufficient coordination between different actors in implementing policies, while communications between civil servants and the public were unsatisfactory. Conflicts between political parties made it more difficult to find appropriate solutions. "Ministers have the power to appoint people for administrative positions in their ministries who are not professional public servants. These are undoubtedly political figures, whose appointments depend on political party considerations" (Hesse, 1993, 228). Because of the political nature of some high-level appointments in the Czech Republic and the reality that professional careers depended on the goodwill of ministers, these public servants' role as the guardian of propriety and the legal framework was significantly limited. The Government's perception of the world was distorted by political ideology, which prevented politicians from viewing situations as they arose impartially.

The instability of the state authorities, on whom the modification of the administrative, judicial, and political apparatus depended after 1989, contributed to the unsatisfactory status of public administration. Many active representatives of the former regime were forced to leave. The newcomers who replaced them often had inadequate education, experience, and moral sense to perform their new tasks successfully. "There is an obvious lack of expertise and morality among government representatives, many of whom solely pursue personal gain" (Cejp, 1995, 13)

Even after the changes in 1989 one of the most constant and painful problems of public administration has been the ineffectual but gradual expansion of bureaucratic structures.

Example:
At the beginning of the 1990s just under 3,000 posts were assigned to the Ministry of Defense to oversee the 300,000-strong Czechoslovak army. By 1995 the Ministry of Defense staff had risen to 3,500, while the army had shrunk to 80,000 (Rašek, 1995, 17).

It seems clear that some of the arguments put forward against government intervention in economic activities were marshaled with the sole purpose of enabling their authors to hide their profit-making activities behind unclear legislation and to further neutralize the already practically nonexistent governmental controls.

Analysis of the organizational structure, function, and working style of the Czech state since 1989 shows that the new regime has consistently utilized the state apparatus handed down from the communist period.

Examples:
Numerous crucial measures of public administration reform have not been introduced since 1989. These include the following: (i) Reform of public administration at the regional level, including the introduction of intermediary self-administrative bodies between central and local governments. This was written into the Constitution of the Czech Republic in 1992 and has still not been implemented. (ii) A law on the civil service which would codify fundamental aspects of the character of public administration, especially its professional character, impartiality, public control, and methods of evaluating its internal and external effectiveness. (iii) Increasing the prestige associated with public servants and precisely defining their associated rights and obligations, political and social position, and career and salary advancement possibilities. (iv) Creating recognized university-level education programs in public administration. (v) A series of laws to establish a system of management for public administration and independent interior and exterior controls—including financial penalties—and a supreme administrative court (Vidláková, 1995, 11).

An amendment to the law on the division of administrative competencies, passed after the parliamentary elections in 1996, abolished the Office for Legislation and Public Administration. This office was the only authority empowered to initiate, conceptualize, coordinate, and methodically guarantee reform of public administration at a centralized level, without passing these responsibilities on to another institution.

8. Conclusion

This chapter has illustrated the lack of clarity which characterizes the situation of public servants in terms of power, areas of responsibility, rules of service procedures, and conditions of social protection. It has also probed the harmful politicization of various components of public administration, the slack control mechanisms within government, and the lack of specialized education which would prepare novices to work in public administration (common in a significant majority of advanced countries, and adopted by a number of countries in Central and Eastern Europe, including Poland and Bulgaria, since 1989). The Czech Republic's reluctance to establish the institution of ombudsman, again in contrast to Poland and Hungary, exemplifies many of these issues.

The following points summarize desirable trends for public administration development in the Czech Republic: (i) a shift away from centralization towards functional decentralization; (ii) movement from an authoritarian conception of public administration to one based on service provision for the public—"It is up to the bureaucracy to adopt the attitude of service that should symbolize a system of public empowerment and bureaucratic accountability, not a system of perpetually demonstrating control" (Baker, 1993); (iii) a shift from direct forms of control (directives) to indirect mechanisms (whether positive stimulants or negative sanctions that are threatened or imposed); (iv) the creation of independent internal mechanisms to control public administration; (v) the establishment of institutionalized mechanisms to support a partnership between government, the market, and the civic sector. (For a more detailed discussion of this point, see chapter 9.)

4. The Civic Sector

One feature of the Czech national character is a strong dislike of bureaucracy; [another] distinctive feature is the mystical belief that bureaucracy should care for everything and that it has full access to any and all available means to do so . . . Any duty we take away from government is political progress. The rise of democracy is feasible only in the form of civic autonomy.

Karel Čapek (1993)

1. Introduction

To begin with a terminological remark, a number of other expressions, more or less synonymous, are commonly used in place of the term 'civic sector', including non-profit sector, non-governmental (NGO) sector, and non-profit civic associations and initiatives. Those wishing to highlight the position of the non-profit sector within the confines of the market and government choose the term 'third sector' (Streeten, 1993, 1288). We will use the term 'civic sector' (Brown, 1994) to signify the entire set of institutions that enable citizens to associate with one another for motives other than profit, as well as the conditions and resources created for that purpose. Individual institutions in this sector are called non-profit organizations. Occasionally the term 'non-profit sector', which represents all non-profit organizations but excludes their relationship to the conditions and resources necessary for their activities, will also be used.

2. Defining the Civic Sector

The non-profit sector emerges from the grassroots activities of civil society, which itself evolves from the public's civic attitudes. Etzioni (1988) characterizes citizenship as the moral obligation of individuals to take an interest in the community in which they live. This definition distinguishes citizenship from the technical use of the concept which implies allegiance to a particular government. This obligation encourages people to do something for others. "With the concept of citizenship introduced at home, cultivated in schools, fostered by the news media, enhanced by voluntary associations, and extolled from Presidential and other civic leaders' 'pulpits', the citizens of a nation feel obliged to contribute to the well-being of the community they share" (Etzioni, 1995, 56).

Civil society may therefore be understood as "the independent self-organization of society, the constituent parts of which voluntarily engage in public activity to pursue individual, group, or national interests within the context of a legally defined state–society relationship" (Weigle and Butterfield, 1993).

Civil society propagates itself by means of constantly emerging, functioning, and dissolving social interactions between citizens. It creates opportunities for citizens to collectively express and act upon their opinions and values. Civil society encompasses two basic components: (i) social actors characterized by their civic attitude towards public concerns as defined above: citizenship; (ii) a legal framework defining the relationship between government and self-governing institutions.

Situations may arise in which society has the potential for promoting citizenship, but government does not create the necessary institutional framework for its cultivation and application. Citizens are, therefore, left with no choice but to find alternative means of association in order to realize this potential, or resign themselves to living without it. Prior to 1989 one alternative form of association was Charter 77, created in the former Czechoslovakia in 1977 in order to defend human and civil rights. The regime persecuted members and supporters of this group until communism was overthrown in 1989.

Example:
At the beginning of the 1980s I researched the history of a particular sports club. Formally, it was an institution near the bottom of the hierarchical pyramid of political power. The Communist Party of Czechoslovakia was at the top, followed by the National Front, the Czechoslovak Union of Physical Education (CUPE), and below that the Czech Organization (CO) of CUPE and the District Committee of CO CUPE. The Physical Education Union Spartak in Prague's fourth district fell under the district committee. However, this sports club—which was a traveling team of the Union—had been formed spontaneously in 1968. During normalization several hundred Prague high-school and college students joined this institutionalized community and organized sports games and trips outside the city, as well as various other independent social activities. Among themselves, they never identified their community as anything other than the Gymnasium Club.

The civic sector is the institutionalized expression of the life of civil society. The sector is made up of non-profit organizations which are voluntary associations of citizens who share common values and are willing to work together.

Legal and other conditions which govern the functioning of the civic sector may support and cultivate—or stifle and destroy—the potential for social participation and people's willingness to be involved in creating positive social conditions for themselves and for others.

Non-profit organizations may be distinguished in terms of their orientation: do they seek to meet the needs and interests of their own members, or do they seek to assist others by promoting and fulfilling public interests. Naturally, one focus will dominate the other. It is difficult to find an organization which focuses exclusively on either the public good or limited group interests. In chapter 9 we will see that corporatist institutions are non-profit organizations which work concurrently in pursuit of both group and public interests.

Non-profit organizations form an essential institutional framework which enables citizens to associate and influence public affairs as partners of government and market institutions. Nevertheless, if citizens are not interested in participating, even the existence of appropriate legislation and favorable economic conditions for non-profit organizations will not guarantee the development of the civic sector, nor will society exercise its potential for citizenship and social participation. This is dealt with in more detail in chapter 5.

3. A More Detailed Definition and Classification of Non-Profit Organizations

In a democratic society there are various forms of non-profit organizations. They may be established as: civic associations (including trade unions and political parties); churches and religious societies; foundations (or funds); charities; professional chambers; interest associations of legal entities (founded for non-profit aims); cooperatives (founded for non-profit aims).

The civic sector acts as a nerve system affecting all the organs and tissues that constitute civil society. Non-profit organizations are most often involved in the following types of activities: social care; health care; sports; education and training; associations of social groups with specific interests (including children, young people, women, students, the physically handicapped, and homosexuals, among others); the environment; housing and the development of municipalities; safety and protection of property; culture; hobbies (such as gardening, animal breeding, fishing, hunting, or stamp collecting); human rights for individuals and minority groups; trade unions; professional and specialized associations and chambers; peace and international cooperation; religion; politics.

A team led by Professor Salamon at Johns Hopkins University is conducting long-term international comparative research on the civic sector. In the following section we present some of the conclusions Professor Salamon and his team have reached.

4. Structural and Operational Definitions of the Civic Sector

The civic sector, according to Salamon, is composed of organizations that comply with five fundamental criteria. These organizations are:

(i) Formal: institutionalized to some extent. Purely *ad hoc*, informal, and temporary gatherings of people are not considered part of the non-profit sector, even though they may be quite important in people's lives. As the same time, the non-profit sector may include many organizations that are not formally incorporated. Typically, however, non-profit organizations have a legal identity as corporations chartered under state law. This corporate status makes the organization a legal entity—and therefore able to enter into contracts—and largely frees the officers of personal financial responsibility for the organization's commitments.

(ii) Private: institutionally separate from government. Non-profit organizations are neither part of the government apparatus nor governed by boards that are dominated by government officials. This does not mean that they cannot receive significant government support. Moreover, government participation on non-profit boards is not unheard of, as was the case at Yale University until the 1870s. However, in their basic structure non-profit organizations are fundamentally private institutions.

(iii) Non-profit-distributing: not dedicated to generating profits for their owners. Non-profit organizations may accumulate profits, but they must be plowed back into the basic mission of the agency rather than distributed to the organizations' founders. This differentiates non-profit organizations from the other component of the private sector—business.

(iv) Self-governing: equipped to control their own activities. Non-profit organizations have internal procedures for governance and are not controlled by outside entities.

(v) Voluntary: involving a meaningful level of voluntary participation, either in conducting the agency's activities or in managing its affairs. This typically takes the form of a voluntary board of directors, but extensive use of volunteer staff is also common.

5.   Functions of the Civic Sector

The civic sector exists to fulfill two basic purposes. By its means, people pursue activities in which they are interested and through which they want to realize themselves—the social function. At the same time, political cohesion is strengthened and the political culture of society is developed—the political function. However, the civic sector's contribution to the economy is also growing in many countries: as a consumer, a producer of goods and services, and an employer—the economic function. Because this function may be understood as secondary, let us return to the social and political aspects of the civic sector which are difficult to grasp and to separate from one another.

Frič et al. (1996, 29) divide the social function of the civic sector into service, which is the output and provision of specific services, and participation, which encompasses the need to associate, actively contribute to the activities of an organization, and have influence. The civic sector offers people an opportunity to choose how they will participate in community life and provides a means of self-actualization through immediate, familiar, and non-formalized social contact and cooperation—the opposite of the superficial, formal modes of human contact which prevail in many aspects of societal life.

The political function of the civic sector is characterized by Kjarum (1992). "Non-profit organizations fulfill a dual role in democratic society. They not only create the foundations of civil society, but also support both the constitutionally defined political process and the existence of formal democratic political institutions . . . The key function of non-profit organizations is to interpret citizens' requirements. They do so by facilitating dynamic citizen participation and raising citizens' awareness of these requirements. Through them, citizens' wishes and needs are articulated, transformed into political demands, and in this way become part of the political process." The political function of non-profit organizations in the development of democracy has become one of the most hotly debated topics of recent times in the Czech Republic.

Opinions differ. Political liberals support only the classic form of representing public opinions, through elections. Some theoreticians, on the other hand, believe that, "in every place where people feel offended or influenced by the effects of a decision, the possibility to inspect and influence the decision should be a part of the decision-making process" (Naisbitt and Aburdenová, 1992).

Both perspectives, one emphasizing the institution of representative democracy, the other emphasizing participatory democracy, are one-sided and insufficient in respect of functioning social processes and relationships. A developed civic sector makes democracy more resilient in the sense that, in addition to the essential traditional channels of representation which define democracy, it offers another way for citizens to articulate their opinions and take action. The civic sector provides citizens with the opportunity to influence public policy more substantially than voting in elections once every few years.

Šilhánová et al. (1996, 7n) and Frič et al. (1996) propose that the civic sector will only function to the fullest extent possible if it supports diversity and the development of different opinions, in other words, if it strengthens political plurality. The civic sector gives people an opportunity to gain political experience, with the understanding that this experience could later be applied in 'real' politics. It also creates mechanisms that allow for the timely detection of internal or external threats to democratic principles in a given country. Brown (1994, 6) concludes that there may be, "enormous benefits for democracy that accrue when this sector is strong and well organized".

6.   Resources of the Civic Sector

How effectively the civic sector manages to join the stream of social activity depends to a great extent on situation and context. One resource is extraordinary events which shake people's consciousness and serve as catalysts in the formation of new non-profit organizations and civic initiatives.

Example:
Fedor Gál (1994, 94n) describes the tragic death of Filip Venclík in 1993, one of many cases characterizing the growth of violent crime in the Czech Republic. This event brought into being an initiative called the Movement for Citizens' Solidarity and Tolerance (the Czech acronym is HOST). Its mission is to monitor manifestations of fascism, racism, and violence, publish the results, and provide services—especially legal—to victims of violence. Vlastimil Venclík, Filip's father and a founder and spokesman of the initiative, says, "As a result of my personal tragedy, I now know what real human solidarity is. There are moments in life when you feel that no hope remains and everything seems to be in vain, [and] when solidarity and empathy help you to go on living and overcome despair."

Gál (1994, 95) concludes that civic movements evolve in areas in which people see problems and are motivated to confront them. Fundamental social changes, however, such as those currently occurring in the Czech Republic, have the potential to weaken non-profit organizations by making the public and private sectors appear more attractive.

Example:

The transformation which commenced in 1989 brought economic stress, the need to adapt to changing conditions, and the possibility of achieving previously unimaginable degrees of self-realization. This made people less interested in some non-profit organizations, particularly those that functioned as substitutes for organizations which had been officially prohibited during the communist era. After November 1989 the most active members of these organizations moved from the non-profit sphere to careers in politics and public administration, a development which negatively affected the civic sector. A clear example is the movement of many environmentalists from the Czech Union for the Preservation of Nature or the Association of Ecologists at the Czech Academy of Sciences into high positions at government ministries or in the Parliament. This brain drain has had a lasting impact. The Czech Union for the Preservation of Nature is still short of qualified young activists at all levels (Damohorský, 1995, 19)

A second important 'resource' of this sector is a legal framework codifying the inception, activities, and financing of non-profit organizations, including government support of the sector (in the form of advising, training of personnel, information services, and so on).

Many countries provide advantages to publicly beneficial non-profit organizations, including tax breaks and other benefits. Organizations that serve primarily their own members or whose membership consists of a closed circle of people are not eligible (Šilhánová et al., 1996, 7). Tax benefits for sponsors and non-profit organizations are, of course, an indirect means of government support of the civic sector. On May 22, 1996 Robert Dole, a Republican presidential candidate in the USA, addressed this topic: "Tax breaks for people who decide to financially support foundations fighting poverty represent a middle road between the apathy of public administration on the one hand, and a lack of concern by the public for social problems on the other." In addition, government earmarks some financial resources from the public budget for the activities of non-profit organizations. This, however, can bring a host of problems.

Example:

When non-profit organizations were declared legal entities in the Czech Republic after the fall of communism in 1989, their dependence on donations from the government budget decreased and their own income increased, which has elevated their non-partisan nature and independence from the government. However, reliance on government contributions still continues "at the expense of objectivity of expression and free speech, because it makes organizations censor themselves" (Damohorský, 1995).

The final important resource non-profit organizations have at their disposal is their internal organizational potential. Their success in achieving their aims and the rationality with which they manage their finances depend in large part on the capabilities and experience of their leaders and members.

7. Strengths of the Civic Sector

The civic sector is more effective than the market and government in activities that: generate minimal or no profit; demand compassion for the needs of others and a willingness to help them; need a holistic approach; provide immediate and sensitive assistance to individuals (such as daycare, advisory services, or assistance to the ill or handicapped); assume considerable trust on the part of clients; require volunteer involvement; gain financial support through grants; encompass moral criteria and individual responsibility.

John McKnight (cited in Osborne and Gaebler, 1992, 66) presents the following differences between services provided by professionals and those provided by informal associations (in this case the definition is very broad—it encompasses not only non-profit organizations, but also the family and neighborhood). Associations of this kind: are more committed to their members than service delivery systems are to their clients; understand the problems better than service professionals; 'solve problems', while professionals and bureaucracies 'deliver services'; provide 'care', while institutions and professionals provide 'service'; are more flexible and creative than large bureaucracies; are less expensive than service professionals; enforce the standards of care they provide more effectively than bureaucracies or service professionals; concentrate on encouraging clients to solve their own problems, while service providing systems substitute for the client's own motivation

In the language of economists the civic sector is best suited to act when the comparative transaction costs of regulating and carrying out the activity would be unreasonably high if the market or government were to intervene.

Publicly controlled non-profit organizations which support initiative and enterprise while searching for ways to cover their own costs combine the strengths of government institutions with those of businesses. In this way they may avoid the shortcomings of both and be the most effective institutional alternative. The word 'may' is used here intentionally because it is also possible for these institutions to embody the typical pitfalls of both government and the market.

8. Shortcomings of the Civic Sector

The theoretical literature on the shortcomings of the civic sector is relatively sparse. Nevertheless, several characteristic situations in which non-profit organizations typically fail have been identified.

8.1 Insufficient Capacity for Dealing with Extensive Tasks

The informal nature of the civic sector, though advantageous in many situations, can become a disadvantage when it is necessary for a large number of people to make a significant, long-term effort. A disciplined and professional governmental apparatus or determined rent-seeking can be more effective in these situations. This is common in smaller, informal organizations, whereas traditional, well-established organizations that depend less on volunteer work (such as schools or hospitals) have a better chance of successfully avoiding this shortcoming.

8.2 The Absence of Necessary Civic Initiatives

One of the appeals of the civic sector is that it allows citizens to become involved in matters they consider to be important. Sometimes, however, group interests differ from the public good. If public administration relies too heavily on cooperation with the civic sector it may sometimes be unable to find a suitable partner.

8.3 Heightened Sensitivity to the Personal Characteristics of Participants

Mutual trust is the tie that binds citizens who participate in civic associations or initiatives. Internal conflict can be devastating for such organizations; the personalities of leaders in these organizations pose an especially large threat. They may tend to usurp power or manipulate the organization to their own ends, particularly if control mechanisms are undeveloped or weak. Even non-profit organizations are not immune to the dangers of oligarchy.

8.4 The Threat of Bureaucracy

The means—implementing the non-profit organization's programs through administrative activities—are sometimes transformed such that administrative activities become an end in themselves.

8.5 Insecurity and Instability of the Civic Sector

Although some non-profit organizations make significant contributions to society over an extended period of time, others are fragile institutions which cannot guarantee that they will survive long enough to satisfy responsibly either a significant segment of the public interest or the needs of their clients.

8.6 A Screen to Conceal the Profit Motive

When non-profit organizations operate in a legal vacuum—that is, the legal framework for their activities is insufficient or fails to monitor their economic ventures—it is possible to abuse the system. The 'public good' can become a front behind which non-profit organizations hide illegal profit through tax evasion or unreasonably high honoraria.

9.　Development of the Civic Sector in the Czech Republic since 1989

Rose (1996) compares the power structure of functioning socialist societies to an hourglass. A basic level of trust exists among the politically powerful, supported by the common privileges they have attained. Likewise, trust based on daily face-to-face contact exists between the politically powerless. A narrow channel connects these two groups, which generally explains the widespread distrust and the feeling that life is a matter of 'them and us'. Society is atomized in a way that requires the power structure to be fundamentally separated from the powerless masses. A supportive mechanism called 'mobilized participation' is provided by organizations similar to the former Czech National Front, which subordinates all forms of citizen associations to political supervision and a strong administrative framework (Weigle and Butterfield, 1993). In societies with a developed culture of citizenship, on the other hand, power structures take the form of a pyramid. Trust between the political elite and citizens is based on wide, horizontal connections between people, which link individuals and political representatives by means of numerous civic sector institutions. The horizontal trust that exists on all levels facilitates and strengthens the vertical trust between people who are affected by public affairs and those who are temporarily entrusted to take charge of them. "Civil society—in this context, the articulation of its [own] interests by society independently of the state—was public enemy number one for a system that required social atomization as a necessary condition for its survival and reproduction, and that did virtually everything in its power to prevent the types of social, political, and economic interactions that could promote individual and group autonomy" (Schöpflin, 1991, 241).

The postcommunist countries have inherited highly fragmented and atomized societies with a significant lack of trust among individual citizens, not to mention between individuals and government. This heritage, encoded in values and patterns of behavior, is being overcome slowly and with difficulty. People are not used to associating or working to protect their interests when they are threatened. Government representatives are not used to negotiating with representatives of interest groups or with the public. Successful contact between these groups is sporadic and incidental, rather than systematically or legally established. There is the constant risk of inappropriate actions from both sides, stemming from a lack of information or understanding. In this context, non-profit organizations can play an important role as institutions capable of shaping the behavior of their members through control, stimuli, and moral conviction. They extend the amount of time available to participants in order to reach agreement, thereby increasing the stability and reliability of social relationships.

The attitude of postcommunist governments towards the civic sector is extremely important. Government has the power to contribute to the 'resources' of the civic sector by purposefully and systematically passing suitable legislation and creating a favorable political atmosphere which promotes civic sector development, and by providing public money to support this sector—either from the state budget or by introducing favorable tax concessions for sponsors and non-profit organizations. The government's willingness to use this power is the main issue.

The following quote is taken from a speech made on March 2, 1995 by Václav Klaus, Prime Minister of the Czech Republic from 1992 through 1997, and presents the Czech Government's view of the civic sector during the decisive transformation period:

> There is a constant search for something that is neither a society of 'atomized' individuals nor a bureaucratic state. History has shown innumerable times that no path leads there, but rather that freedom, political pluralism, and the market are the best tools to create a just, civilized, and solidaristic society. This conviction has driven my four-year polemic in favor of the market alone, of a standard system of political parties without national or civic movements, and, based on the same logic, has also directed my actions to create a *society of free citizens*, rather than the misleading idea of a *so-called 'civil society'* [Klaus's emphasis] . . . What is 'civil society'? I am afraid that it is something more than a society of free citizens, that collectivism is somehow attached to individualism in this society, based on the perception that this somehow complements and improves the basic principle of citizenship . . . The natural, voluntary association of citizens in various unions, clubs, and associations is an elementary mark of a society of free citizens who do not live like Robinson Crusoe on a desert island. There is no need for social reforms or 'civil society' for that, nor for innovative theories that promote the idea that the value of association or community should be more highly prized than the value of freedom. Associating is a logical consequence of the existence of groups of citizens with similar interests. Nevertheless, it is a consequence of their own interests, which sometimes enrich society and sometimes do not. Therefore, the impact these associations and their activities will have cannot be known in advance. A group of citizens will undoubtedly promote its interests more easily than each citizen alone, but this is not and cannot be perceived as a positive in every circumstance. In order for that to be true, we would have to believe the optimistic hypothesis that people do not promote their own interests, but rather work towards higher values which enrich society. The validity of this hypothesis is not supported by any evidence. Therefore, proponents of so-called civil society should not rely upon it. (Klaus, 1996, 288–91)

As a theorist, Klaus presents himself as an orthodox neo-liberal, both economically and politically. He presents himself as a methodological individualist, denying the need to analyze human forms of association by any means other than the examination of the intentions and actions of individuals. Klaus even disputes the ontological status of human communities and repudiates the idea that people would associate for any reason other than self-interest. As a theorist, he may have the right to believe this. However, these are not just the beliefs of one individual. They had a substantial impact on the policies of the Czech government while Klaus was Prime Minister. One clear manifestation of this was the Government's never-ending reluctance to adopt new legislation regarding non-profit organizations, a legislative vacuum which made their position very uncertain in the period from 1989 to 1995 (Damohorský, 1995, 30), and significantly impeded the transformation of many important sectors, including education, health care, social security, physical education, and municipal services.

Josef Jařab, who has served both as a senator and rector of a prestigious university in the Czech Republic, is convinced that the strongest party of the government coalition, the Civic Democratic Party, attempted to stunt the development of civil society in the Czech Republic after 1989:

> [civil society] is a concept with a long tradition. It is impossible to imagine any Western democracy, particularly the United States, without civil society. The goal of civil society is not to dilute governmental power, as some of our politicians wrongly perceive, but rather to encourage public participation. A citizen is not just someone who votes once every four years. There is also a need for self-realization through participation in non-governmental organizations and citizen associations, whose objectives are not only the members' private interests, but also more common interests. These activities create the political, cultural, and social climate of society . . . If we have not matured sufficiently in the last seven years as citizens, it is partly because nobody has led us in that direction. People develop into citizens only when they have an opportunity to do so. (Jařab, 1996, 30)

The Czech law on publicly beneficial organizations finally came into force, after many delays, on January 1, 1996. Due to the continued absence of a special law, however, it was still very easy to establish a foundation and, due to inadequate and unclear tax regulations, it was possible to misuse this institutional form to evade taxes until the law on foundations was accepted in the fall of 1997. In addition to other non-profit organizations, the legislation affects the position of churches which are still fighting for restitution of their former property and for separation from the state in order to gain economic independence (Novotný, 1995).

Šilhánová et al. (1996) and Frič et al. (1996) provide data on the number and field of activities of non-profit organizations in the Czech Republic. According to these studies, in 1989 there were slightly more than 2,000 registered civic associations (including organizational units, chambers, interest associations, and foundations). After 1989 their number rose significantly: by the end of 1992 there were more than 20,000 non-profit organizations, and by 1996 there were nearly 37,000, of which approximately 4,500 were foundations. These figures are approximate not only because central statistics were not kept, but also because many of these institutions exist only on paper. The majority of civic associations are traditional organizations, including sports clubs (11,700 of them in 1996), hunting associations (5,000 in the same year), and parents' clubs (about 2,700). The increase in registered organizations after 1989 is to a significant extent due to the fact that a majority of sports clubs and hunting associations were active before 1989 but were not registered independently, since only national umbrella organizations were listed. Similarly, parents' clubs (which grew out of the now defunct Association of Parents and Friends of the School) were newly registered as independent entities.

Even assuming that 37,000 non-profit organizations existed in 1996 the resulting rate of less than four non-profit organizations per 1,000 inhabitants is low in comparison with developed democracies. According to reliable estimates 100,000–150,000 people in the Czech Republic work in non-profit organizations, 2–3 per cent of the total work force. Their activities account for approximately 1 per cent of GDP. This is also low in comparison with Western countries: in the United States, for example, the civic sector accounts for 5–10 per cent of GDP.

Based on these data it seems that, despite the statistically remarkable development of the civic sector in the Czech Republic in recent years, we cannot be sure to what extent it is an 'optical illusion'. There is, however, a positive dimension to this careful, even pessimistic statement. It demonstrates that there is, without a doubt, great potential for the civic sector to develop further. This potential is examined in chapter 5, partly on the basis of evidence drawn from public opinion polls.

5. Citizens

1. Introduction

Citizens both create and are affected by the regulators of social life discussed in the previous chapters. They represent the key element in any consideration of the mechanisms and outcomes of regulations because politicians' beliefs regarding their motivations, dispositions, and tendencies may fundamentally influence the choice and utilization of individual regulators: the reactions of citizens to the actions of politicians often correspond to how closely these beliefs coincide with reality. An analysis of the functioning of the market, government, and the civic sector would therefore not be complete without considering the behavior, attitudes, and value orientations of the population.

Academics who study society (sociologists, political scientists, economists, and jurists) sometimes come to rely so heavily on their theoretical schemata that they persuade themselves that their fellow citizens are prepared to comprehend and take in the world around them according to these schemata, too. This is a crucial error. While academic journals are full of 'transitional' explanations about the move towards democracy and the market economy in postcommunist countries, ordinary people perceive the world mainly on the basis of their daily worries and experiences. These two worlds are dependent on one another to a certain extent: people relate to that part of a given academic explanation that is conveyed to them by politicians and the media. Experts, if they like, are able to analyze systematically how 'the people' view current issues. For politicians, careful analysis of public opinion can be a decisive factor in determining their political actions.

One vision of politics which has emerged in the Czech Republic since 1989 is based on the possibility and necessity of enhancing public concern with society and citizens' responsibility for public affairs: in other words, civil society. This chapter examines the extent to which that vision has been fulfilled. Additionally, we look at changes in the employment of individual regulators and in the policies implemented in the Czech Republic since 1989. Findings are presented which demonstrate the significance of these changes, as well as the manner in which they have affected the opinions and actions of citizens. We will also look at the development of people's behavior and their attitudes towards different institutes and aspects of public life—among other things, what people think about the market, government, and the institutions of the civic sector.

This chapter is based primarily on the results of empirical research conducted in order to learn the opinions of Czech citizens and local self-governments concerning public policy (henceforth: "our research"). The research was made in 1995 within the framework of a study entitled 'An Analysis of the Process of Formation and Implementation of Public Policy in the Czech Republic After 1989', completed at the Faculty of Social Sciences of Charles University, Prague, and supported by the Grant Agency of the Czech Republic.[1] The group was composed of 1,007 citizens and 222 local self-government representatives. In order to compare and analyze development trends this chapter also refers to other empirical research into citizens' opinions conducted by Czech public opinion research firms, including STEM, IVVM (the Public Opinion Research Institute), and GfK. Further considerations are based on average values which characterize the whole research sample, or a portion of it, which make it possible to consider the results as approximating the real composition of opinions throughout the adult Czech population. With some exceptions this book does not examine or lay out specific characteristics of social or demographic groups.

2. Behavior and Actions

Immediately after the collapse of communism and the creation of the basic legal conditions for business activities, there was an enterprise boom. Within a short time over one million independent entrepreneurs were registered (although not all of them gave up their regular jobs), and tens of thousands of new firms were created. This shows that people understood the opportunities presented by business activities carried out independently in the market, which in the official economy prior to 1989 had been forbidden. Furthermore, in response to the newly developing capital market a substantial majority of citizens participated in two waves of voucher privatization.

This led to an exceptional degree of mobility in the work force which had not been possible in previous decades. Estimates show that between 1989 and 1995 more than one-half of all economically active individuals changed jobs. Of course, this was not always voluntary but resulted from changing employment conditions: as the economy evolved many unnecessary jobs ceased to exist. Other departures, however, meant an active choice: a search for opportunities more closely in line with people's interests.

It is possible to conclude from this that most people were capable of responding flexibly to the introduction of market mechanisms.

One of the generally recognized indicators of an active interest in public life is participation in elections. In the Czech Republic, however, we see a declining trend. In 1990, 97 per cent of eligible citizens voted in parliamentary elections; in 1992 the figure had fallen to 85 per cent; and in 1996 it stood at 76 per cent. Even worse was to come: in November 1996 only 35 per cent of eligible voters participated in the first round of elections to the newly formed Czech Senate. However, it is important to realize that in the wake of the political changes at the end of the 1980s voters saw elections as a referendum on the new regime. In this sense, the decrease in voter participation may be taken as a mark of stability: people were no longer afraid that democracy might come under threat. This confirms other research which follows the development of public opinion regarding the solidity of the new political order. At the same time, voter participation is still substantially higher in the Czech Republic than in many other established democracies.

Membership of a political party is not common in the Czech Republic. The enforced 'voluntary' participation of the last regime made this kind of civic activity unattractive to many people—at the very least they are suspicious of it. Membership is not high either in the newly established political parties or in those restored after November 1989. The Civic Democratic Party, the strongest party in the government coalition in both 1992 and 1996, was able to claim only 20,000 members in 1996 and had local associations in less than one-quarter of Czech cities and communities. The second strongest party after the 1996 parliamentary elections, the Czech Social Democratic Party, had 14,000 members. One coalition partner, the Civic Democratic Alliance, and other smaller parties had even fewer members. The Party of Pensioners for Life Security, on the other hand, claimed to have 30,000 members. Significantly higher membership could be claimed by only two parties, both of which were established before November 1989. In 1996 the Communist Party of Bohemia and Moravia had 300,000 registered members and the Christian Democratic Union–Czechoslovak People's Party had a membership of 70,000.

3. Attitudes

People's attitudes are influenced by how they understand and interpret the conditions in which they live. As already mentioned, attitudes are strongly influenced by propaganda, advertisements, and ideologies offered by the media and prominent politicians. *Sub specie aeternitatis*, however, people are most likely to be decisively influenced only by their own life experiences and the opinions of their friends and acquaintances. Therefore, it is important to devote more attention to what citizens consider to be urgent issues in public life.

The main theme of the present book is the role of the basic regulators—the market, government and its institutions, and the civic sector—in people's lives. Because of that, it is important to consider how people perceive them and the values which are usually associated with them. Citizens' political orientation is loosely affiliated with their perceptions of these regulators. The research on which many of the following conclusions are based also examined the degree to which people's satisfaction and dissatisfaction are influenced by politics.

4. Evaluating the Problem Areas of Public Life

In repeated independent public opinion surveys citizens were asked which issues they considered to be the most important and how satisfied they were with the ways in which these issues were being addressed in the Czech Republic. Analysis of the resulting data led to the classification of problems into four groups, ranging from 'very urgent' to 'not urgent'. The degree of urgency is a function of public perception of a given problem and dissatisfaction with how this problem was being handled by government and other responsible authorities.

4.1 Very Urgent Problems

These were (i) the fight against crime and (ii) corruption (incorporating the conflict of public and private interests, and money laundering). Both sets of problems are linked with rapid institutional changes—including the development of a market economy, a disrupted system of values, and a weakening of the conception and control function of public administration. They are exacerbated by a distinct imbalance between the regulatory power of government and the market. The market invaded space which had previously been government regulated. Its strength was not successfully contained, so it flooded its banks and wreaked havoc wherever it flowed.

4.2 Urgent Problems

The most frequently listed were: social security reform; environmental issues; care for families with children; housing; health care for citizens; schools and higher education. These are issues for which serious political economists recommend the support of long-term public sector investment, with the goals of cultivating human capital and protecting the environment. As with the first set of issues, however, the government's myopic emphasis on economic reform and the establishment of free-market institutions meant that people's needs in this category were not satisfied, which was immediately apparent to the population.

4.3 Less Urgent Problems

These included: minority issues (that is, nationality and the Roma people); unemployment; economic reform, including market development; and the development of a democratic political system. This group contains issues which were at the center of attention for representatives of the new regime, but the problems 'were not perceived as urgent' by the population. The sole exception is the chronic failure to resolve sensitive issues related to national minorities, which was not a priority for the government.

4.4 Problems Not Viewed as Urgent

These were: the defense capabilities of the Czech Republic; support for Czech culture; the development of cities and regions; informing citizens about public affairs; and supporting self-help and non-profit organizations. This final group includes problems which do not affect the majority and so are not felt to be urgent by most people. The final three issues, however, are closely related to the creation of the conditions necessary for the development of civil society.

Generally speaking, people are more interested in issues that directly threaten or improve their living conditions. Successes or failures linked with the development of independent mechanisms of political democracy, the market economy, and civil society cannot be a priority because the positive or negative impacts of these issues are only rarely directly connected with people's everyday problems.

As public opinion has evolved since 1989, issues related to economic reform, unemployment, and education have gradually become less urgent. On the other hand, housing and health care reform have become the main focus of attention. The fight against crime, threats posed by criminals and the mafia, and the existence of corruption have remained the largest and most constant problems for Czech citizens since the beginning of the transformation in 1989.

5. Attitudes towards the Market and Government

The available data only indirectly indicate the importance and value attributed to the market and government by ordinary people. However, even on this basis it is possible to arrive at some interesting conclusions. A number of public opinion polls have gathered information about the public's preferred ways of managing the economy (Table 5.1).

Table 5.1 Type of Economy Preferred by Citizens (%)

Type of economy	1993	1994	1995
Socialist	5	9	10
Social market	59	53	60
Free market	36	38	30

Source: STEM Research.

A socialist economy was characterized by the authors of the poll as an economy run by a centralized government, such as the one which ruled the Czech Republic until 1989. In a social market economy government influences the economy mostly in an indirect way, but also by redistributing resources. In a free market economy the state plays a minimal role. Although this research only considers the relationship between government and market in the economic sphere, citizens clearly prefer a solution in which neither the state nor the market has all the power. A significant segment of the population supports even extreme versions of a socialist type of economy.

Our research in 1995 brought to light important findings concerning public opinion in relation to public policy. Among other things, we asked respondents if they agreed with the following statements:

1. "I am in favor of the kind of freedom which allows people to decide for themselves, act in their own interest, and be responsible for themselves."

When the viewpoint was formulated in this way, 83 per cent of respondents agreed, 11 per cent disagreed, and 6 per cent did not know.

2. "I am in favor of the equality of citizens insofar as: (i) no one has unauthorized advantages or disadvantages, and (ii) the government provides support for socially or physically handicapped people."

This statement received approval from 87 per cent of respondents, while 8 per cent disagreed, and 5 per cent did not know.

This leads us to the conclusion that a majority of Czechs are liberal as long as they can rely on state support in difficult situations. Nearly three-quarters of respondents agree with the concepts of freedom and of social equality. Only one-tenth of respondents are decisive proponents of freedom and adversaries of equality, while only one-thirteenth are in favor of equality at the expense of freedom (Purkrábek et al., 1996, 5n).

It is difficult to interpret this conclusion. One possible explanation of it is that Czech society has, thus far, avoided stratification to the extent that people still find both freedom and equality within their own areas of experience (which implies that people who are more dependent on the state prefer equality, while people who perform well in the market prefer freedom). By contrast, my hypothesis is that Czechs understand that both equality without freedom and freedom without equality are undesirable—and that the market and government are able to complement one another in many situations.

Example:
A majority of citizens are convinced that, in the sphere of housing, the government should intervene in the market to a certain extent in order to create more suitable conditions for poor households: "As evidence that the majority of people prefer that government play a greater rather than a smaller role in the sphere of housing, take the fact that fewer than half of respondents agree with the statement, 'Housing is primarily the private affair of each citizen'" (Valentová in Purkrábek et al., 1996).

This interpretation corresponds with the political orientation of the Czech public in relation to the spectrum of political values and ideologies. The same stable trend has been visible in numerous public opinion polls conducted over the last several years: approximately two-thirds of citizens hold centrist opinions, while extreme positions are held by only a few. Twice as many people have a clear rightist orientation as have a leftist one, although this tendency has been slowly decreasing since 1995: in opinion polls on public policy since 1995, 14.1 per cent of respondents have had a distinct leftist orientation, 63.1 per cent have been centrist, and 22.9 per cent have been distinctly rightist. IVVM research since August 1996, though admittedly not completely comparable, nevertheless shows an aggregate shift towards the center. The results were as follows: 9 per cent leftist, 71 per cent centrist, and 20 per cent rightist. In both cases, percentages were calculated on the basis of the total number of respondents who stated their political orientation.

New conditions, especially the revitalization of the market and private initiatives, have created a *nouveau riche*. Confidence in the market as a legitimate regulator of societal life is, to a certain degree, predetermined by the existence of conditions which favor the widespread interpretation of new wealth as legitimate and deserved—in other words, that the beneficiaries of the market have achieved concrete and visible results in circumstances of equality for all interested participants. The image of the *nouveau riche* is documented in Table 5.2.

Table 5.2 Opinions of the Czech Public Concerning the *Nouveau Riche* (%)

Money was earned through hard work	17	Money was earned easily	81
Property was gained honestly	26	Property was gained dishonestly	73
Did not take advantage of others to get rich	31	Got rich by taking advantage of others	69
Got rich thanks to a position they created for themselves in the current regime	45	Got rich thanks to their position in the previous regime	53

Source: GfK Research (1996).

These results show that people are preoccupied by such practices as the gaining of economic advantage through political position, corruption, money laundering, organized crime, and other illegal methods of attaining wealth. This reflects an extremely dangerous tendency—the failure of government to regulate the market, to the extent that it could threaten people's confidence in the entire reform process. This failure could even lead some of the population to the conclusion that the reintroduction of an authoritarian state is necessary.

6. Attitudes towards the Civic Sector

Responses to the key question 'What is the potential for citizen participation in the Czech Republic?' presuppose a comparison of: the actual participation of citizens in civic sector activities; an as yet unrealized preparedness to contribute to the activities of this sector; and obstacles that have prevented citizen participation in this sector in the past.

The Czech public does not attribute great importance to the existence of non-profit organizations. Among seventeen areas of public policy which were rated by citizens in public opinion polls the support provided by non-profit organizations was viewed as the least important (Table 5.3).

Table 5.3 The Importance of the Civic Sector in the Eyes of Citizens and Local Government Representatives, 1995 (%)

I consider the support of self-help and non-profit organizations for myself and my friends to be:	Citizens	Local government representatives
Decidedly important	8	13
Probably important	16	22
Not important but not unimportant	32	34
Probably unimportant	13	14
Decidedly unimportant	7	4
I don't know	24	13

Source: Results (1995).

One-quarter of citizens had no opinion about the role of non-profit organizations. The level of awareness of the importance of the civic sector is higher among local government representatives, evidently because they often meet people who are active in the sector and are therefore exposed to the results of its activities. The nature of the public's view of the civic sector, including whether it is perceived as a specific, relatively homogeneous sector of public life, remains an open question. Frič (in Purkrábek et al., 1996) hypothesizes that people are aware of non-profit organizations which were transformed after 1989 and are oriented primarily towards traditional leisure activities. However, these organizations are most likely not perceived as being part of the civic sector, which is associated mainly with recently created organizations, particularly foundations and citizens' associations, which address 'new' problems, such as drug abuse, the handicapped, runaways, or the homeless.

The perception of the role of civic organizations, primarily movements of various kinds, is becoming polarized. The public has a positive view of ecological initiatives (such as Children of the Earth, Rainbow, and Greenpeace) and human rights movements (Committee for the Protection of the Unjustly Accused and the Helsinki Citizens' Assembly). On the other hand, it is strongly opposed to skinhead and anarchist movements. According to IVVM research from June 1996 the percentage of respondents who considered the activities of skinheads and those of anarchists to be decidedly harmful was 86 per cent and 75 per cent respectively. The activities of human rights movements were judged to be decidedly or probably beneficial by 71 per cent, while ecological movements received this rating from 73 per cent of respondents.

Opinions on trade unions and the tripartite institution (whose role is to serve as a forum for the trade unions, the Government, and the employers) are characterized in Tables 5.4 and 5.5.

Table 5.4 The Czech Public's View of the Role of the Trade Unions, 1995 (%)

Trade unions are relics that are complicating the rapid transformation to a market economy	8
Trade unions should solely advocate the interests of their members	16
Trade unions should advocate the interests not only of their members, but also of other employees	40
Trade unions should not only advocate the interests of employees, but also participate in decision-making about wider political issues	28
I don't know	8

Source: Results (1995).

Table 5.5 The Czech Public's Opinion of the Usefulness of the Tripartite Institution, 1995 (%)

It is definitely useful and desirable and should deal with broader issues of social policy as well	41
It is useful up to a point but should involve itself solely with issues related to labor relations, working conditions and wages	34
It is more or less useless	6
I don't know	19

Source: Results (1995).

A majority of Czechs are in favor of the activities of both trade unions and the tripartite institution—only a small proportion of surveyed citizens have a clearly negative attitude towards them. This is a significant finding which is clearly important in respect of decisions regarding the role of corporatism in the development of the Czech political system. (For more information, see chapter 9.)

7. Attitudes towards Public Administration and Institutions of Representative Democracy

The nature of the public consciousness is to a certain extent linked to its attitudes towards institutions of government and political democracy. This attitude is a real expression of the prevailing sense of citizenship as it indicates the public's identification with political conditions and its willingness to play a personal role in implementing policy.

It is clear that public faith in the powers-that-be was deeply undermined during the years of totalitarian rule. It was a case of 'them and us', the two sides divided by a deep gulf of mistrust and misunderstanding. What was the relationship of citizens to government and its political institutions six years after the reemergence of democracy (Table 5.6).

Table 5.6 The Czech Public's Confidence in Government Institutions and Political Democracy, 1995 (%)

Institution	Confidence	Lack of confidence
President	63	15
Prime Minister	33	32
Local and city representatives	32	19
Supreme Accounting Office	28	21
Ministry of Finance	23	33
Courts	21	35
Ministry of the Environment	18	31
Ministry of Education	16	39
Ministry of Defense	14	31
Ministry of Labor and Social Affairs	14	43
Parliament	14	45
Ministry of Health	12	50
Ministry of the Interior	9	45

Source: Results (1995).
Note: Remaining respondents answered "half and half" or "I don't know".

Confidence, rather than lack of confidence, characterizes the relationship of citizens to the President, local and city representatives, the Supreme Accounting Office, and the Prime Minister. People have less confidence in the ministries, and particularly low confidence—and even a marked lack of confidence—in the Ministries of the Interior, Health, Labor and Social Affairs, and Education. Parliament also stands low in the public esteem (the ratio of those lacking confidence in Parliament to those who have it is 3:1), as do the courts (which are supposed to be the arbiters of impartiality and the guarantors of rights in all circumstances). Other independently obtained research results confirm these findings. This is alarming when one considers that a properly functioning Parliament and court system are the institutionalized embodiments of democratic ideals.

Slightly more satisfaction than dissatisfaction was expressed concerning the work of district and municipal authorities and self-governments; satisfaction increased and dissatisfaction decreased in respect of the administration and representatives in the election period after 1994.

These data are confirmed by research conducted by IVVM. In July 1996, 55 per cent of respondents had confidence in the municipal authorities and 26 per cent did not, while during 1994 these percentages more or less evened out (46 per cent and 43 per cent respectively).

The public administration's contact with citizens frequently leaves much to be desired: this concerns both its professionalism and impartiality and the manner in which it deals with citizens (Table 5.7). Leaving behind the approach characteristic of the previous 'authoritarian' administration and coming to understand public administration as a service for the benefit of citizens seems to be beyond the capabilities of many, if not most, Czech public servants.

Table 5.7 Satisfaction with the State Authorities' Approach towards Citizens, 1995 (%)

Characteristics of administration and administrators	Satisfied	Dissatisfied
Professional knowledge	22	30
Organizational skills	18	33
Culture of client-oriented behavior	20	38
Impartiality in decision-making	16	36
Personal readiness to assist in solving problems	18	44

Source: Results (1995).

Example:
IVVM regularly surveys the public concerning access to justice and citizens' rights. Those questioned with regard to administration have little hope in this connection and estimate their chances after several years as 'small' or 'rather smaller than greater' (between 1993 and 1996 between 55 and 75 per cent of respondents gave one of these two answers). Optimists who estimate their chances as 'great' or at least 'rather greater than smaller' are in the minority, their number varying between 17 per cent and 36 per cent. Problematic contacts with the administration or the powers-that-be is the most frequently cited obstacle.

---

8. Potential for Citizenship in the Czech Republic

Throughout the political and economic changes which have occurred in the last few years insufficient progress has been made in the direction of the integration of the powerful and the powerless. This is paradoxical given that today the powerless are undoubtedly in a much better position to control and influence the actions of the powerful than they were in the past. One statistic says it all: in 1995 almost two-thirds of citizens (62 per cent) held the opinion that nothing prevented them from influencing the outcome of public affairs (Results, 1995, 39).

There are a number of causes of the indisputable deficit of citizenship—of active participation in the life of society. One of them is evident in the behavioral stereotypes characteristic of Czech society: after the long decades of communist rule people have forgotten how to 'speak up'. A second is the economic stresses of transformation which have forced people to concentrate first and foremost on earning a livelihood. A third important factor is that traditional channels of social control and mechanisms of representative democracy have not reacted quickly and effectively enough to the needs of the majority. Finally, the Czech govern-ment, which has largely concentrated on the economic aspects of transformation within the framework of its neo-liberal dogma, has not acknowledged the importance of purposefully building up (albeit from scratch) the infrastructure of civil society, represented by the civic sector.

The foundations of civil society have already been laid, but it is not a good idea to depend on initiatives coming from the top. In chapter 4 (on the civic sector) we showed that citizen initiatives can—and often do—break down the walls of administrative ignorance. Nevertheless, let us pose a hypothetical question. What would happen if measures were taken to build up an adequate infrastructure for civil society? Would this development opportunity be utilized?

Fewer than half of all citizens are prepared to participate directly and personally in public affairs (Table 5.8). Higher than average interest is typical of men, people aged between 40 and 60, the educated, and residents of smaller municipalities. Significant interest was also noted in people who have experienced changes in their social position since 1989, regardless of whether it has risen or fallen. Intensive interest in politics and public affairs is shown by less than one-tenth of adult citizens.[2]

Table 5.8 Interest in Personal Involvement in Public Affairs, 1995 (%)

Response	Men	Women
Yes	40	27
Probably, not fully decided	22	23
No	33	41
I don't know	5	9

Source: Results (1995).

Individual citizens' responses as to why they would not be interested in participating in public affairs ranged from subjective (time constraints accounted for 34 per cent, age for 14 per cent, and different political views for 5 per cent) to objective obstacles—mistakes of democracy were cited by 17 per cent, the administration's lack of interest and corruption by 10 per cent, and the fact that individuals were former communists and therefore prohibited from public life by 2 per cent (Results, 1995, 40).

Representatives of local administration and self-government offer another perspective on the willingness and motivation of citizens to participate in public affairs. Citizens' lack of interest in the activities of the municipality, according to 74 per cent of local government representatives, is one of the biggest problems that they encounter in their work. (The only problem cited more often was insufficient financial resources for developing the municipality, which was listed by 84 per cent of respondents.) Other problems are perceived to be much less pressing (Table 5.9).

Table 5.9 The Czech Public's Attitude towards Municipal Affairs in the Opinion of Public Administrators, 1995 (%)

Not at all interested in the activities of the municipality	6
Criticize but are unwilling to do anything themselves	55
Show initiative only when it is in their personal interest	28
Help out whenever necessary	5
Other and "I don't know"	6

Source: Krumphanzl in Purkrábek et al. (1996).

Table 5.10 compares the current and potential participation of citizens in the activities of various civic sector organizations.

Table 5.10 Willingness to Participate in the Activities of the Following Organizations, 1995 (%)

Organization	Do	Want to	Want to, but cannot	Do not want to
Voluntary cultural, physical training, and other leisure time organizations	20	14	23	43
Voluntary organizations providing services to the public	6	16	29	49
Environmental movements	4	18	28	50
Human rights movements	2	18	23	57
Professional associations	13	11	16	60
Trade unions	13	7	13	67
Local self-government	5	9	19	67
Government administration (i.e., commissions)	5	6	16	73
Church or religious organizations	7	5	7	81
Protest movements or single protest actions (strikes, petitions)	5	9	4	82
Rightist-oriented political party	3	4	8	85
Centrist-oriented political party	2	5	8	85
Leftist-oriented political party	3	3	5	89
Nationalist political movement	1	1	2	96

Source: Results (1995).

This illuminates many aspects of both current participation and people's willingness to become active in public life. Traditionally, most people take part in the activities of voluntary sports and cultural organizations, trade unions, and professional associations. Within these organizations the potential for further and wider participation is limited: trade union membership has been falling for the last several years. Lower participation and less participatory potential is also visible in respect of churches and religious organizations. Our research discovered low current participation, but a high interest in future participation in charities, human rights, and environmental movements. "The high number of currently passive but interested people [allows us to infer] that citizens' involvement in the Czech Republic will be oriented towards non-traditional spheres of public life" (Frič in Purkrábek et al., 1996).

The relation of citizens to local self-government and, surprisingly, to public administration is characterized by a higher rate of latent interest than actual participation. Traditional political parties and nationalist movements attract weak citizen support both currently and potentially. (From IVVM research we may conclude that only 19 per cent of citizens over 18 were convinced followers of a political party at the beginning of 1996. This percentage has consistently declined since May 1990.) The greatest potential for development in this sphere is for centrist-oriented political parties. The general political mediation of interests simply does not attract participation as much as the opportunity to work towards the realization of specific interests, whether private or public. This is an additional argument for the cultivation of elements of corporatist democracy as a functional complement to representative democracy. (A more detailed discussion of this problem may be found in chapter 9.)

At this point it is necessary to highlight the paradox that, while public activity does not seem to attract many people, they are still aware that politics greatly affects their lives (Table 5.11).

Table 5.11 Impact of Politics on Feelings of Personal Satisfaction, 1995 (%)

Decisive	15
Great	34
Neither great nor small	27
Rather small	12
None	9
"I don't know" or "I can't judge"	3

Source: Results (1995).

Despite the fact that three-quarters of those asked believe that politics can have a substantial impact on their personal satisfaction or dissatisfaction, only a small portion have decided to influence the political process themselves by directly participating in public affairs. There are a number of logical explanations for this. Many people do not believe that they have a realistic chance of influencing the impersonal, shortsighted, and difficult control mechanisms for creating and implementing policy. Others hope that this responsibility will be shouldered by others.

This situation should be perceived by both politicians and political scientists as an urgent challenge. Many people are prepared to enter public life and actively participate either in politics or another form of public administration. They do not do so, however, because the institutionalized forms for mediating such participation seem inaccessible. At the same time, they clearly sense the insensitivity to their needs of the political parties, the ungracious way in which the public administration treats citizens' concerns, and the difficulties of establishing and running non-profit organizations.

Changes for the better will not come automatically. One prerequisite is a change in the markedly reserved attitude of Czech government representatives towards reforming public administration and stimulating the development of the civic sector. Without decisive political support a significant portion of the potential for citizen participation will remain untapped.

6. Values and Ideologies

1. Values and Ideologies and Their Relationship to the Regulators

No analysis of the role of the market, government, and the civic sector would be complete without at least a brief consideration of human values and political ideologies. The value context creates a milieu in which the mechanisms we have been considering are implemented, and which is influenced in turn by their functioning. Several arguments support this hypothesis. One is that every regulatory mechanism's effectiveness increases when it corresponds closely to the characters and value systems of a significant number of people. Second, the choice of regulators is strongly conditioned by ideologies which influence political decisions and the way that people think. Third, these regulators create the social environment for people and are echoed in the development of their values. Finally, human efforts and desires may be projected onto a vision of what is desirable—the regulators are only instruments by means of which they may be achieved. Even possible 'choices of society' are significantly determined by people's value orientations. These arguments are explored in more detail in the following section.

Could the market or government function without considering individuals' value orientations? Take the following examples. A prerequisite for market success is the identification of individuals who are interested in exchanging goods. However basic this prerequisite may be there are extreme cases of people who live exclusively from charity or stealing. If everyone acted in this way the market would collapse. Another example is the pursuit of narrow self-interests without considering the public good: a ship on the high seas will reach its destination only if the sailors obey their captain. If every sailor decided to stop working, relax, and squander the supplies the result would almost certainly be the demise of everyone on board. And is not society a ship on whose safe arrival the fate of the passengers—citizens—depends?

A further, functional argument supports the necessity of socially accepted values. If citizens agree, at least on a basic level, on what is desirable for a given society, that society may be managed more easily and inexpensively: it is necessary to expend far fewer resources than would otherwise be the case to prevent activities that could threaten the desired aims, and fewer positive stimuli or threats are necessary to coordinate people whose activities contribute to the public good (Arrow, 1974; Etzioni, 1991).

On the basis of a comparative study of a number of societies (including Japan, the United States, China, Germany, and Italy), Fukuyama (1996) came to the conclusion that the market is a necessary but insufficient condition for economic success. The other necessary condition is the mutual trust of actors entering the market and their willingness to cooperate with one another—in other words, social capital. Without trust the gears of the economic machine stick and supplementary sources are required to cover additional transaction costs in the form of ever increasing rules, regulations, and sanctions.

Many others, including Engliš and Mlčoch, have analyzed the moral foundations and preconditions necessary for an economy to function well. Mlčoch (1994, 16) contends that "no economic system may be founded solely on self-interest".

Fromm (1994) examines the third argument cited above, concerning the manner in which the social regulators create the social environment. He shows that personal character and value orientations may change as a result of stimuli generated by social conditions. His criticism of capitalist society is based on the conviction that the accumulation of material assets which it requires increases the importance people place on the possession of things—having—and leads them to neglect cultivating themselves as individuals—becoming. Tawney (1952, 33–34) says that capitalist society "assures men that there are no ends other than their ends, no laws other than their desires, no limits other than that which they think advisable. Thus, it makes an individual the center of his own universe and dissolves moral principles into opportunistic behavior."

The influence of institutions on human values is not characteristic only of the market. We need not look far to see other examples: poorly functioning state socialism in the Czech Republic clearly demoralized people, who developed a tolerance for both greater and smaller deceptions, and learned to live double lives, both public and private. Cejp (1995, 12) views the totalitarian regime's impact on the value systems of individuals and society between 1938 and 1989 in this way: "The structure of traditional civil society was degraded, and the institutions of the family and the school [the function of which was] to raise children, as well as the institutions of the legal system and the police [the function of which was] to protect citizens, were crippled."

As a bearer of values and cultural traditions religion was discouraged. The activities of religious institutions, such as Catholic charities, which provided citizens with social and health care services, were curtailed or stopped completely (Novotný, 1995). From the communist era we inherited repressed and limitless aggression, insufficient respect for ordinary civil 'rules of conduct', and a seriously demoralized society. The liberalization of economic life has taken place in an environment in which laws and ethical norms do not apply.

During the period of transformation, therefore, it is necessary to expect a shortage or outright lack of the internal norms which regulate human interaction. At the same time, it is important to realize that, while some norms do exist and have an impact, they do not necessarily work in harmony with the demands which are changing the structure of the fundamental regulators—the market, government, and the civic sector.

2. Values

Every consideration of values is based on a particular understanding of human nature and a definition of humankind's position in the world. Therefore, before discussing the advantages of a particular political measure, we require clarification concerning a number of concepts of human nature, motives, and other factors which influence human behavior in the network of social relationships.

In the European cultural context the Judeo-Christian tradition has played a major role in forming value systems and people's relationships to one another by means of ethical codes such as the Ten Commandments. Charity, an integral part of Christian teachings, led to the creation of many social institutions for the purpose of helping people in difficult life situations. Catholicism has developed this tradition over the last century in the form of Christian social teachings (Spiazzi, 1993).

Bentham proposed the utilitarian ethic in an attempt to ground all moral values on the benefits which derive for an individual from a given action. The fulfillment of individual interests was for Bentham a means of achieving the greatest happiness for the greatest number of people. Mill expanded this concept to include promoting the well-being of others. He was a proponent of positive state intervention in the market to promote social well-being, which he understood to be the sum of the well-being of all individuals.

A significant contribution to the understanding of human beings was made with the differentiation between possible and actual human conduct, between latent possibilities of individual self-realization and the manner in which this possibility is actualized. This spiritual tradition grew from Aristotle's concept of essence, the view that human development is a process of gradually moving towards the ideal form.

Renaissance humanism joined this spiritual tradition. Nicolaus Cusanus developed the concept of 'unfolding' human capabilities—the latent strengths slumbering in human beings which are utilized only under particular social and economic conditions.

Analysis of the development of abilities generally concentrates on what people can do or be. Desirable development is understood as an emancipation process from an initial state of enforced non-being, of 'living less or being less', rather than as a process of expanding the range of goods and services. Human beings may choose diverse life alternatives by focusing on their developing abilities. The range of possible alternatives depends on an individual's characteristics and on surrounding social conditions.

In the second half of the 1980s the concept of 'hidden human potential' related to social, economic, and political conditions was introduced in Czechoslovakia as a theory of human potential (Potůček, 1991; 1992). Human potential was defined as that component of the perceived human tendency to act and exist in relationships which develops human beings and society. This theory encompasses such areas of human potential as health, the ability to learn, proficiency, value orientation, individual integration and regulation, social participation, and creation.

In our examination of the relationship of values to the market, government, and the civic sector, several key values will be considered. Most important for this discussion are the extensively discussed values of freedom, equality, and human rights. Theorists of the 'new right' such as Nozick (1974), the Friedmans (1980), and Hayek (1976) defend the view that freedom and equality are incompatible: "As long as the belief in 'social justice' determines political actions, this process inevitably brings us ever closer to a totalitarian system" (Hayek, 1976, 68n). This viewpoint is fundamentally rejected by egalitarian theorists who maintain that the values of freedom and equality are indeed compatible.[1] Worthy of attention in this connection is evidence from public opinion polls that three-quarters of the Czech public favor the values of freedom and equality equally, as we discussed in chapter 5.

Currently, the relation of social conditioning to individual development is being addressed by a number of theorists, including Sen. In order to understand the development of human capabilities it is necessary to differentiate between negative and positive freedom. Negative freedom focuses on the absence of barriers by means of which individuals or institutions may constrain one another. Positive freedom concentrates on what individuals are or are not able to achieve: " If we consider it important for people to be able to live life according to their own choices, the general concept we must address is that of positive freedom" (Sen, 1990, 49). Positive freedom is defined as a broad spectrum of possible choices: "It is quite possible that, were an illiterate person taught to read, he or she would still decide to read nothing . . . It is a fact that a great many people do things that others do not do. Nevertheless, that does not make it irrelevant that people sometimes choose the same thing with equal benefit" (Sen, 1984).

Theorists interested in the concept of human resources are also concerned with understanding the complexity and mutual conditioning of human, economic, and social development: "The evolution of human beings into educated, motivated, healthy, and well-fed individuals is not merely a final goal, but also a necessary condition of productive work and economic development" (Streeten, 1989, 74).

No analysis of the problems of the industrial age may ignore the important issue of human rights. The concept of human rights that has been employed frequently since the beginning of the twentieth century evolved from the earlier concept of natural rights. The first theorists of natural rights—Grotius, Hobbes, and Locke—placed particular emphasis on the rights to freedom and the possession of property. The concept of natural rights was first incorporated into a political document in 1776, in the form of the Declaration of Independence of the United States of America: "We hold these truths to be self-evident, that all men are created equal, that they are endowed by their Creator with certain unalienable rights, that among these are life, liberty, and the pursuit of happiness."

The French Declaration of the Rights of Man of 1789 spoke of inherent, inalienable, and irrevocable rights. This calls to mind the slogan of the French Revolution: "Liberty, equality, brotherhood." These are directly linked to a host of human rights declarations, the most significant being the Universal Declaration of Human Rights which was adopted by the General Assembly of the United Nations in December 1948.

This school of thought evolved not only a different view of the status of individuals in society, but also an emphasis on liberal freedoms that formed the foundation on which democratic political systems and public policy were built. It made possible the introduction of the market and the subsequent unprecedented blossoming of the economic sphere. On the other hand, it also paved the way for the emergence of totalitarian movements which, in the name of equality, succeeded in subjugating entire societies at the cost of enormous suffering.

Human rights may also be derived and defined on the basis of human needs which are recognized as fundamental. Marshall (1963) explains the evolution of modern states by linking an elementary form of human equality to the full participation of individuals in the life of a community. This equality is not incompatible with economic inequality.

It is therefore necessary to broaden the concept of citizens' rights to include three components: (i) civil rights, (ii) political rights, and (iii) social rights. Civil rights are connected to individual freedom and consist of the protection of individual integrity, the right to own property and conclude business contracts, the right to justice guaranteed by an independent judiciary, and freedom of speech, thought, and expression. Political rights allow individuals to participate in the functioning and exercise of political power, either by voting representatives into power or having the right to be elected to political bodies. Social rights represent the right of individuals to share in a given society's social inheritance and the right to live with dignity, that is, to live at a level corresponding to prevailing social standards. Marshal claims that, while civil rights were articulated in the eighteenth century and political rights in the nineteenth century, social rights have been defined in the twentieth century.

Let us now consider whether it is possible to derive a correlation between these values and the three main regulators of human activity analyzed in the present volume (Table 6.1).

Table 6.1 Relationships between Values and Forms of Regulating Human Activity

Value	Form of regulation
Negative freedom	Market
	Government, through indirect regulation and enforcement
Human dignity = positive freedom = equal opportunity	Government, through indirect regulation and redistribution of resources
Absolute equality	Government, through enforcement
Responsibility for the fate of society	Civic sector
Solidarity, responsibility for the fate of other people	Family, civic sector, government, through indirect regulation and redistribution of resources
Transcendental responsibility	Churches, as part of the civic sector

Contemporary societies are characterized by a plurality of opinions concerning what is and what is not right and desirable. Much evidence supports the belief that this plurality is the bearer of a necessary range of possibilities which promote adaptability in difficult situations. On the other hand, every society needs a common denominator, a core that respects and conveys the decisions of the majority to citizens, in order to keep the society from dissolving.

3. Ideology

Public policy as social practice should be based on a foundation that facilitates the communication of what is, what should be, and what is no longer the public good or in the public interest. This foundation would give meaning to the different choices that are put to citizens and politicians, and could guide daily decisions in decisive or important situations. Therefore, we should ask ourselves what sort of comprehensive value systems are at our disposal and how they can be applied within the framework of the 'established' market, government, and non-profit organizations.

Some political ideologies, along with human values, significantly influence decision-making in the market, government, and the civic sector as the main regulators of human activity. These are relatively general, comprehensive interpretations of social problems and possible means for resolving them, and are evaluated according to the differentiated social interests of various groups of citizens. However, they also include communal or social interests, that is, public interests.

Table 6.2 Positive Relationships between Ideologies and Selected Values

Value	Ideology				
	Neo-liberal*	Conser-vative	Social liberal	Social democrat	Totalitarian (fascism, communism)
Negative freedom ('freedom from')	Yes	—	—	—	—
Civil rights	Yes	Yes	Yes	Yes	—
Political rights	Yes	Yes	Yes	Yes	—
Responsibility for the fate of society	—	Yes	Yes	Yes	—
Solidarity (responsibility for the fate of others)	—	Yes	Yes	Yes	—
Positive freedom ('freedom to') = equality of opportunity	—	Partial	Yes	Yes	—
Human dignity	—	—	Yes	Yes	—
Social rights	—	—	—	Yes	Yes
Equality	—	—	—	—	Yes

* The term 'liberal' is used here in the European sense to express a rightist affiliation—trusting the market and mistrusting government.

The following section looks at the interrelationships between the regulators and these doctrines and values, and then examines how the latter have influenced decision-making in the market, government, and the civic sector in the Czech Republic in recent years.

The value foundations of individual doctrines are characterized in a schematic way in Table 6.2.

Table 6.3 describes the relationship between ideologies and forms of regulation. Neo-liberal and totalitarian doctrines (communism, fascism and so on) are once again at opposite ends of the spectrum. For neo-liberals, the basic component of society is the individual pursuing his own interests, the ideal arena for which is the market. For proponents of authoritarian regimes, on the other hand, the needs of the whole are primary and the desires of individuals must be subjugated. The ideal means of enforcing totalitarianism in society is the state. Conservative ideologies emphasize traditional institutions such as the family and the Church. They are not against the market, but tend to apply both indirect regulators and direct governmental enforcement functions in areas that might threaten the disruption or destruction of the functioning of the social organism. Social democratic doctrine is compatible with a successful market, but also tends to strengthen limited group (class) solidarity. Civil and political rights must not interrupt the fulfillment of social rights. For social liberals, individual freedom, civil rights, and political rights are undeniably the most important. However, limiting the market and supplementing its regulatory function with other methods of regulation, particularly indirect forms, is also considered a viable way of fulfilling the criterion of equal opportunity. Social liberal, conservative, and social democratic doctrines are favorably inclined towards social regulation by means of non-profit organizations which they view as legitimate ways of expressing and realizing the varied components of group and general societal interests.

Table 6.3 Relationships between Ideologies and Forms of Regulating Human Activity

Value	Ideology				
	Neo-liberal*	Conservative	Social liberal	Social democratic	Totalitarian (fascism, communism)
Individual	Yes	Yes	Yes	—	—
Market	Yes	Yes	Yes	Yes	—
Government:					
(i) through indirect regulation	Yes	Yes	Yes	Yes	Yes
(ii) through redistribution of goods	Yes	Yes	Yes	Yes	Yes
(iii) through enforcement	—	Yes	—	—	Yes
Civic sector	—	Yes	Yes	Yes	—
Churches viewed as non-profit organizations	—	Yes	—	—	—

Ideologies, or political doctrines, are necessary components of communication in political discourse in that they facilitate identification of political perspectives and priorities. However, ideological frameworks oversimplify the understanding and interpretation of social reality. When confronted with a difficult situation they are a potential instrument of misunderstanding and can be used to justify unreasonable and irrational decisions and actions.

This situation demonstrates the advantages of political pluralism, which facilitates the free exchange of opinions and a range of political preferences. It also promotes the identification of misleading or deforming elements that sometimes cannot be perceived through an ideological screen, and before policy is actually implemented. It provides a mechanism for changing and correcting existing ideologies when necessary in the face of new and previously unknown problems. Political pluralism helps government address tasks such as battling international terrorism, while it allows non-profit organizations to raise consciousnesses and, for example, to arouse a sense of self-preservation in the face of human society's increasingly negative influence on the environment.

4. Ideologies and Regulators in Czech Society in Recent Years

The official ideology of communist governments was Marxism–Leninism, which gave government nearly absolute power, while the market and the independent civic sector were repressed. This barrier was definitively overcome in Central and Eastern Europe in 1989. Gabal (1996) notes that the need to establish broad-based foundations for civil society and a moral renaissance were basic aspects of political development in the first months and years after 1989.

In the political life of Czechoslovakia from November 1989 through the second free elections in June 1992, social democratic, social liberal, and neo-liberal ideologies co-existed and supported one another. The concept of societal transformation implemented by the government elected in 1992 was based on thoughtful consideration of the functions of the institutions of political democracy, the market economy, and civil society.

The 1992 election brought with it a significant change. Supporters of neo-liberal ideology won the battle for political power, which led to the implementation of a narrowly focused transformation concept, a one-sided preference for the market, accelerated economic reforms, and the systematic underrating of the role of government and the civic sector in influencing society. The neo-liberal ideology positively influenced society by helping to break down recalcitrant state institutions inherited from the past, giving legitimacy to new approaches and measures, and successfully implementing radically different policies (Potůček, 1994b).

With the benefit of hindsight, however, it is possible to assert that it was counterproductive to narrow the aims of social transformation and to degrade "politics and civic life in order to serve the needs of economic transformation, its success, and a solidified power position for political forces linked directly with economic transformation and indirectly with privatization" (Gabal, 1996, 7). In the end, this was reflected in the parliamentary elections of 1996, in which broad support was expressed for more balanced concepts related to the values of freedom and equality. The narrow market concept typical of the theory and practice of the neo-liberals lost many of its previous supporters. The collapse of the right-wing coalition government led by Václav Klaus at the end of 1997 is additional evidence to support this claim.

7. Seeking a Balance

> Among the dichotomies that hinder serious intellectual examination, few are as detrimental as the notion that free markets are 'good' and governments are 'bad'.
>
> *Amitai Etzioni (1995)*

1. Introduction

This chapter explores the relationships which exist between the market and government, between government and the civic sector, and between the market and the civic sector. In light of this, it compares the characteristics, strengths, and shortcomings of the individual sectors and examines ways in which they may co-exist.

2. The Market and Government

2.1 Changes in the Relationship between the Market and Government

Needless to say, history offers numerous examples of widely differing relationships between the market, government, and the civic sector.

Example:
Slavery was a very desirable institution from an economic point of view because it reduced the costs of labor to a minimum. On the other hand, the slaves were forced to endure miserable living conditions. A gulf of inequality separated them from free citizens, thus weakening society's basic sense of justice. The recognition of universal human rights by governments resulted in the abolition of slavery, which had an immediate impact on the nature of the job market. Increased labor costs understandably handicapped enterprises which had previously profited from slave labor.

Given the course of industrial evolution over the last 100 to 150 years it is surprising how significantly the role of government in people's lives has increased in comparison with that of the market. "The prevailing developmental tendency has been to expand public projects. Many projects were carried out by specific communities and gradually became associated with them, which made it increasingly difficult for individuals to perform the same tasks in the market" (Hendrych, 1992, 14).

The share of public spending in the GDP of developed countries has increased consistently since the beginning of the twentieth century and currently stands somewhere between thirty and fifty per cent of the total. Although attempts are sometimes made to explain this development as exclusively the result of subjective political will, it is primarily an evolutionary development, resulting from the increased complexity of society. The need to provide people with various public goods cannot be left solely to the free market.

Even neo-liberally oriented theoreticians are unable to contest a—perhaps irreplaceable—role for government that the market cannot play. For society to function well it is necessary for government to manage justice and public administration, defend human rights and freedoms—including important property rights—safeguard free elections, and protect society from internal and external threats. Many such theoreticians, however, question the need for government to play a role in any other area of social life: "History has shown us innumerable times that . . . liberty, political pluralism, and the market are the best aims a just, fair and united society can seek to accomplish" (Klaus, 1996, 288).

The processes of industrialization and urbanization have gradually forced governments to organize, finance, and—in some circumstances—manage programs in areas in which it has not traditionally been active.

Example:

In all developed industrial societies, education is understood to be 'capacity building'. In a given set of circumstances a better-educated population is likely to contribute to greater economic efficiency. It is therefore in governments' interest to support education. The same is true of health, which is presently understood to be a good that must be accessible to all.

Other than in exceptional situations, such as war, social services supported, directly funded, or provided by government are the largest 'consumers' of public financial resources. Welfare states have blossomed since the end of the Second World War. Neo-liberals blame these welfare states for many inefficiencies: not merely their deleterious effect on the management of financial resources, but also their tendency to weaken the work ethic and to reduce people's inclination to try to manage life's difficulties with their own means.

Example:

The Conservative government of Margaret Thatcher in Great Britain attempted systematically to limit public spending for social purposes. Empirical analysis shows that she was able to accomplish this within a relatively short time. In the long run and measured in terms of absolute outputs, however, she succeeded only in the area of housing. Both total outputs in this sector, in comparison with prices, and the relative share of public spending in GDP continued to grow. Part and parcel of the neo-liberal approach of the Conservative government was an effort to reduce the regulatory functions of government to a minimum. It became clear, however, that when government gave up part of its role in financing and/or providing public services its regulatory role generally increased. While water, gas, electricity, and telecommunications were provided by the state it was not necessary to regulate their production and distribution nearly as much as it is now, when the British government must

> organize and finance the activities of agencies—OFWAT (the water watchdog), OFGAS
> (gas), OFTEL (telecommunications), and so on—that exist solely to control and regulate the
> private companies active in this field.

Lindblom considers the feasibility of fundamentally changing the role of the market and government in ensuring greater equality of income distribution among individuals. The hypothetical pure market would undoubtedly exacerbate inequality in incomes from salaries, rents, interest, and profit because individuals could depend only on what they could offer for exchange in the market. However, the effects of the modern market are modified by taxes, public expenditure, and other regulatory mechanisms. It is easy to imagine a functioning market that would distribute wealth more equally than is generally the case today.

One argument against this is that decreased differences in income reduce the motivation to work productively. The opposite can also be true: as it becomes more difficult to earn additional income, people work harder. How individuals act depends upon their subjective preferences in respect of work and leisure time, which in turn depend on culture, personality, and many other patterns of social and employment organization which either support or dampen motivation. The market does not intrinsically preclude greater equality of income and wealth than currently exists; the barrier is rather an historically inherited and politically maintained inequality of individually held assets, salary levels, and shares in income. In principle, governments may redistribute income and wealth as often as they wish. Their failure to do so is the result of political choices rather than economic forces.[1]

Sojka and Konečný (1996, 34) claim that, according to economic theory, government carries out three functions in relation to the market. It: (i) ensures the necessary conditions for the proper functioning of the market mechanism by minimizing the negative effects of monopolies, removing negative externalities or compensating for them with positive ones, and maintaining a sufficient amount of public goods; (ii) protects the proper functioning of the market by redistributing resources in order to preserve or establish greater equality of incomes and wealth; and (iii) maintains the economy's internal and external stability by means of macroeconomic stabilization policies.

2.2 Market and Government—An Uneasy Partnership

Lindblom shows that, within the framework of various social arrangements, politics and economics are interdependent (Table 7.1). One of his noteworthy discoveries was the fact that, while market economies may or may not be governed democratically, democracies cannot exist without a market, and centrally planned economies require an autocratic political system.

Table 7.1 Types of Political and Economic Systems

Economic system	Political system	
	Democratic	Authoritarian
Market oriented	Democratic capitalism	Market oriented, but without guaranteed human and civil rights
Centrally planned	------	Socialism

Source: Adapted from Lindblom (1977, 161).

The fact that the market is not an automatic guarantor of democracy is evident in the majority of countries in the world which have functioning markets but lack democratic governments and operational civic sectors: "Market economies can co-exist with one-party rule. Although reforms leading to the implementation of a market economy may safeguard the existence of specific groups and individual interests, they do not necessarily lead to democracy" (Batt, 1991, 33).

Example:

A comparison of the strategies and progression of reform in China and the former Soviet Union—later Russia—illustrates the difficulties that may be caused by rapid institutional changes in the functioning of government (in these cases, the progression from autocratic regimes to governments with an element of democratic choice) if it cannot rely on corresponding changes in behavioral patterns.

The Russian people after seventy years of communism are atomized, disoriented, and unfamiliar with the practices of democracy. Basically, they were not prepared for the emerging political freedom and the greater responsibility for their own fate which accompanies democracy. Western consultants convinced the Russian leadership that so-called 'shock therapy' was necessary: they should destroy the existing economic and political foundations of power in the hope that unlimited *laissez-faire* capitalism would rapidly invigorate the country. Instead, we have witnessed political turbulence, several years of economic depression, and the blossoming of a range of socially pathological behaviors, including organized crime, corruption, and other forms of criminality. (This issue is discussed in more detail in chapter 10.) Tens of millions of Russian citizens now live below the poverty level.

Whatever the motivations behind the strategy chosen by China it seems to have been more effective from an economic standpoint. The Chinese leadership chose an evolutionary approach: they have maintained state institutions at the central and regional levels, and, within the framework of a carefully implemented economic policy, have supported enterprises in the private sector by, among other things, opening the doors to foreign investment. Another important factor in China's economic development is cultural: strong family ties have ensured the maintenance of trust within communities, which was essential for the emergence and prosperity of new family businesses.

This example shows that "the advice of economists to politicians necessarily ignores certain aspects that are important to consider in forming and implementing policy. These recommendations suffer from one-sidedness in that they lack a comprehensive vision of the goal of the transformation process"

(Rausser and Johnson, 1993, 673). In the process of transformation government cannot allow the market free rein without risking unacceptable difficulties. Do any general reasons exist to justify the maintenance of the role of government in market regulation, besides those related to transformation? Ernst Gellner (cited in Musil, 1996, 31) believed that "the side-effects of unlimited economic activity would destroy everything—the environment, cultural heritage, and human relations. These powers simply must be politically restricted, though the control should be gentle, camouflaged, and negotiated. The economy must be strong enough to create pluralistic institutions, but not strong enough to destroy our world."

This brings us back to the relationship between the market and democracy. As has frequently been demonstrated, not all societies with market economies are democracies, but all democracies are market oriented. It is a common characteristic of the market and democracy that they support plurality—in one case economic, in the other political—and make possible the realization of diverse interests. Democracy needs the market as its partner to provide citizens with free choice.

In democratic, market oriented societies the regulatory role of government is not at all simple. Government depends on the private sector in many respects. Because public economic functions—such as maintaining employment, prices, production, growth, the standard of living, and the economic affluence of individuals—are often performed by private business people, government tends to be indifferent to the manner in which the latter achieve their goals. As a result, business people in general—and corporate management in particular—can find themselves in a privileged position in relation to government, a position incomparable with that of any other group, with the possible exception of the civil service. The risk of government failure grows as decision-makers find themselves increasingly bound by distinct interest groups with specific agendas (Mlčoch, 1997, 157).

The contemporary dualism of administration is reminiscent of the medieval dualism of church and state. The relationship between government and business is no less complicated.

Government and business interact in the following ways: government oversees and regulates entrepreneurial activities; implementation of government regulations is limited by consequences that could negatively affect the public functions of business; government is limited in other areas of public policy due to the possible negative impact of given regulations on the business sector; business representatives actively promote their own interests in negotiations with government representatives, and even resort to the threat of decreased economic activity if their demands are not met; business people hold a privileged position, being both passive participants and influential with regard to government decision-making; hypothetically, government has the authority to deny business particular privileges or even to liquidate an enterprise or entire business sector.

A significant symbiosis characterizes the relationship between government and business in terms of which neither side would gain from threatening the basis of the relationship. Although business does not get everything it would like from government it generally has little cause for complaint.

The market cannot function without competition. Competition is, however, a form of conflict. Government is the only institution that has the power to create specific control mechanisms to keep this conflict within boundaries: if government fails, this otherwise productive and constructive conflict may escalate to the point that it destroys the social ties that are a precondition of market exchange, such as trust (Etzioni, 1995, 206–207). Unfortunately, postcommunist countries offer many examples of this type of failure.

3. Government and the Civic Sector

In principle, government may adopt one of three stances toward the civic sector. It can: (i) hinder its creation, eliminate it if it already exists, or subordinate it; (ii) stimulate its development and functioning; or (iii) take no interest in it whatsoever.

The first stance is typical of totalitarian regimes. They attempt to limit the sphere of independent civic life—non-profit organizations are the institutional essence of this independence. The second stance is dominant in societies that are not opposed to the existence of self-conscious and independent citizenship, and where non-profit organizations have already found their niche.

Legislation governing the creation and activities of non-profit organizations varies from country to country. Judging by the many different kinds of non-profit organization such legislation would appear to be beneficial. Besides direct financial support from the public budget, government can assist non-profit organizations by means of tax benefits for the organizations themselves or for private sector sponsors. Historical context plays a significant role in the attitudes of individual countries. In Europe, where strong, centralized governments have ruled for hundreds of years, there is less support for the civic sector than in the United States, which has weaker government and a long history of civic cooperation and philanthropy. On the other hand, in Europe government plays a greater role in financing the civic sector than in the United States, where there is a stronger tradition of support from private sources.

The willingness of the population to take action to resolve particular public problems through the civic sector is also an important consideration. Civic sector activity lightens the burden on government and decreases taxes—in this way civic activism can be said to 'pay off' for citizens. The opposite can also be true: civic 'laziness' decreases the disposable income of citizens because government must take greater responsibility for public affairs. Furthermore, not only is it more costly, it is less effective and less well targeted.

Analysis of the relationship between the civic sector and government in the Czech Republic since 1989 shows three basic development patterns. The civic sector: (i) acts as a substitute for government in areas in which the latter does not function; (ii) complements the functioning of government and sometimes even initiates legislative changes; (iii) is sometimes abused as a means of promoting selfish group interests because of the public administration's failure or lack of responsibility.

In the following section we look at a number of concrete examples of the first two areas of development of non-profit organizations. The third, an example of a civic sector shortcoming, will be analyzed in more detail in the chapter on corporatism (chapter 9) on the basis of the activities of the Czech Chambers of Physicians and Dentists and other health care interest groups.

3.1 The Civic Sector as a Substitute for a Non-Functioning Government

3.1.1 Assistance to Victims of Crime

Help for victims of crime should be provided by government. In the Czech Republic, however, the White Cross Association is active in this area because of the government's absence. With a staff of volunteers it works in crime prevention and provides comprehensive assistance to victims and their relatives. Many other non-profit organizations are also active in this area, including the Salvation Army, Czechoslovak Charter 77, the Czech Helsinki Assembly, the Fund for Endangered Children, the Prevention Crisis Center LOCUS, the Safety Foundation, Drop In, and many others (Cejp, 1995, 21,29)

3.1.2 Care for the Homeless

Their response to the relatively recent appearance of homelessness in the Czech Republic provides clear evidence that non-profit organizations are able to react more quickly than government to new social problems. Shortly after 1989 non-profit organizations began to focus on the increasing number of people without homes. In 1990 the Salvation Army was established in this field and in 1991 and 1992 other organizations followed, including Hope *(Naděje)* and the Diocese of the Evangelic Church of Czech Brothers. Since that time, these organizations have developed to the extent that they are able to offer specialized care for women and children, as well as a number of other services (Vozar, 1996).

The Czech Republic is not the only country in which a functioning civic sector must substitute for a non-functioning government: "None of the American programs of the last forty years which attempted to solve the social problem by means of government action was very successful. Independent non-profit organizations attained notable results" (Drucker, 1993).

3.2 The Civic Sector as a Complement to Government or as an Initiator of Legislative Change

3.2.1 Creation and Protection of the Environment

The Czech Association for the Protection of Nature initiated Law No. 114/1992 of the Czech National Council to protect nature and the countryside. This law "not only contains modern and complex legal norms, but gives citizens' associations the right to participate in forming new laws in the environmental sphere" (Damohorský, 1995, 25).

The public administration would not have been capable of preparing such a law itself. The civic sector—and its members and supporters who were in government during this time—kick-started cooperation between the public and civic sectors with legislative support. However, there have also been failures, particularly in attempts to influence government to pass a law on non-profit organizations and foundations. Disagreement between individual ecological movements weakened their bargaining position with the government, enabling the latter to abort the initiative (ibid.).

3.2.2 Housing Policy
The Housing Association is an umbrella organization which was founded in 1992 in response to the unsatisfactory state of public housing policy. Its members include the most influential agents in the housing sphere—the Association of Czech and Moravian Housing Cooperatives, the Association for the Protection of Tenants, the Citizens' Association of Home Owners, the Association of Cities and Regions, and the Association of the Construction Industry. These associations and their members influence government housing policy—if to a limited degree— mainly through their participation in sessions aimed at influencing the legislative process (Valentová, 1995).

3.2.3 Education Policy
Teachers and other education professionals who are members of professional associations, trade unions, and educational initiatives have actively attempted to influence the formation of education policy. Examples include NEMES, the independent interdisciplinary group for reforming education policy and the education process, and PAU, the Friends of Engaged Teaching. However, these groups have often received a cool reception, at best, from ministerial civil servants (Kalous, 1996).

3.2.4 Law and Order
"As part of the fight against crime . . . it is necessary to encourage citizens' initiatives, associations, and other non-profit organizations, whose goal is to strengthen civil society" (Gabal, 1994, 96). An example of civic initiatives in this sector is the creation and activities of HOST, the Movement for Citizens' Solidarity and Tolerance. This organization's activities are described in chapter 4.

4. The Market and the Civic Sector

There is less friction and resentment in the relationship between the market and the civic sector than there is between either of these sectors and government. This is because they are each dependent, to a degree, on legislation and other conditions created by the state. Businesses and non-profit organizations both stem from private initiatives and so experience similar restrictions and confront similar problems.

The institution of sponsorship is a significant link between these two sectors. By means of voluntary grants business may support the activities of the civic sector and, through its choice of grant recipients, participate in deciding which activities have priority. At the same time, business support for these activities is a powerful public relations tool.

When civic sector activities are not suitably regulated by law and when moral norms are weakened this institutional form may be misused. For example, a business enterprise can assume the guise of a generally beneficial organization in an effort to use the civic sector merely as a cloak for tax evasion and other forms of illegal enrichment. There have been many examples of this in the Czech Republic, undermining the credibility of the entire Czech civic sector.

5. The Simultaneous Functioning of the Market, Government, and the Civic Sector

The overview of regulators and their interrelationships presented thus far makes it evident that their interactions are not without problems. Nevertheless, the collected evidence makes it clear that each sector has strengths and shortcomings, as well as specific domains of activity in which it is effective, and that its effectiveness depends on the extent to which its activities are harmonized with the other sectors.

Tables 7.2, 7.3, and 7.4 compare the basic characteristics, strengths, and shortcomings of regulation that are typical of each sector and provide a basis for considering the ways in which each sector can complement and support, or—on the contrary—weaken and interfere with the others.

Table 7.2 Basic Characteristics of the Public, Private, and Civic Sectors

Characteristic	Public sector	Private sector	Civic sector
Principal mechanism	Bureaucratic organization	Market exchange	Voluntary associations
Decision-makers	Administrators and experts	Individual producers, consumers, savers, and investors	Leaders and members
Rules of conduct	Regulations	Price signals and quantity adjustments	Agreements
Criteria for decisions	Policy goals and the best means of implementing them	Efficiency and maximization of profit and/or utility	Interests of members/ public interests
Sanctions	State authority backed by coercion	Financial loss	Social pressure and/or exclusion
Mode of operation	Top-down	Horizontal contract	Bottom-up

Source: Adapted from Uphoff (1993).

Table 7.3 Prerequisites that Enable Sectors to Provide Services

Criterion	Public sector	Private sector	Civic sector
Public sector strengths			
Stability	Good	Poor	Average
Ability to handle issues beyond the central mission (e.g., affirmative action)	Good	Poor	Average
Immunity from favoritism	Good	Average	Poor
Private sector strengths			
Flexibility	Poor	Good	Average
Ability to innovate	Average	Good	Average
Tendency to replicate success	Poor	Good	Average
Tendency to abandon the obsolete or unnecessary	Poor	Good	Average
Willingness to take risks	Poor	Good	Average
Ability to generate capital	Average	Good	Poor
Professional expertise	Average	Good	Average
Ability to capture economies of scale	Average	Good	Average
Civic sector strengths			
Ability to reach diverse populations	Poor	Average	Good
Compassion and commitment	Average	Poor	Good
Holistic treatment of problems	Poor	Poor	Good
Ability to generate trust	Average	Poor	Good

Source: Adapted from Osborne and Gaebler (1993, 347).

6. Optimizing the Functioning of the Market, Government, and the Civic Sector

In recent years consensus has been growing between specialists in different disciplines that the market, government, and the civic sector play an irreplaceable role in regulating the activities of social actors. Another common conclusion is that it is necessary to cultivate means by which the sectors' effectiveness in resolving pressing problems in communities, countries, and supra-national bodies may be optimized. These authors have been able to draw on past experiences which clearly illustrate that one-sidedness can be deceiving and, at the same time, that human thought and activity can easily be lured down a path that destroys the fragile equilibrium between the regulators: (i) socialism leads many of its champions from a belief in the importance of collective well-being to an overestimation of the role of government as a guarantor of social justice—with a proven negative impact on human liberty; (ii) neo-liberalism (libertarianism), as a school of thought, overwhelmingly endorses the market as the sole regulator of activity. In this way, it threatens a basic premise of modern, stable societies, that is, the creation and sharing of common values, legitimating social order and maintaining social cohesion; (iii) anarchism, with its disdain for state institutions and the market, would prefer to see society self-managed on the basis of pure spontaneity and voluntarism. What institution could be more suitable for this vision of society than the civic sector? The problem, however, is that a functioning market and government are necessary preconditions for its existence.

Table 7.4 Tasks Best Suited to Each Sector

Criterion	Public sector	Private sector	Civic sector
Best suited to public sector			
Regulation	Effective	Ineffective	Depends on context
Policy management	Effective	Ineffective	Depends on context
Enforcement of equity	Effective	Ineffective	Effective
Prevention of discrimination	Effective	Depends on context	Depends on context
Prevention of exploitation	Effective	Ineffective	Effective
Promotion of social cohesion	Effective	Ineffective	Effective
Best suited to private sector			
Economic tasks	Ineffective	Effective	Depends on context
Investment tasks	Ineffective	Effective	Depends on context
Profit generation	Ineffective	Effective	Ineffective
Promotion of self-sufficiency	Ineffective	Effective	Depends on context
Best suited to civic sector			
Social assistance	Depends on context	Ineffective	Effective
Tasks that require volunteer labor	Depends on context	Ineffective	Effective
Tasks that generate little or no profit	Depends on context	Ineffective	Effective
Promotion of individual responsibility	Ineffective	Depends on context	Effective
Participation in the life of society	Depends on context	Ineffective	Effective

Source: Adapted from Osborne and Gaebler (1993, 348).

Historical development is usually not linear, partly because it is influenced by the one-sided doctrines already mentioned. Over time, fundamental changes and even reversals in the strength and interdependence of the market, government, and the civic sector become visible.

Example:
Nationalization of property and the establishment of central planning were fundamental changes that took place at the beginning of forty years of communism in the Soviet bloc. The state confiscated private property and took over the vast majority of the original functions of the market in economic life. In this way, government, itself a tool in the hands of the communist parties, entered without scruple into the domain of the market and attempted to replace or at least to colonize it. At the same time, the autonomous functioning of all parts of the civic sector was made impossible. The negative political, economic, and social consequences of the party state's exaggerated growth—at the expense of the market and the civic sector—are widely familiar. By contrast, since the end of the 1980s Central and Eastern Europe has experienced privatization, adopted the principles of a market economy, and developed an independent civic sector.

History has a tendency to take one-sided solutions—and their protagonists—to their limits, albeit at the price of significant losses and after years, sometimes decades, of confusion. It can be said that ideal and universally applicable relationships between the different sectors do not, and cannot, exist.

Uphoff (1993) is firmly convinced that it is possible to achieve positive synergy between the functioning of the market, government, and the civic sector. In order to transform this hypothesis into a convincing theory, it is necessary systematically to increase our knowledge of how to apply these alternative—somewhat complementary and co-dependent—regulatory tools most effectively. It is especially important to be aware of the cultural milieu, legislative and institutional environment, and quality of human resources and of how they fit into the context of global development trends, threats, and opportunities. The final chapter of this book attempts to apply this hypothesis to Czech society by incorporating general knowledge of developments and problems in different areas of public life since 1989.

The remaining chapters of the book deal with themes that more specifically delineate and clarify the relationship between the market, government, and the civic sector in the transformation of countries in Central and Eastern Europe, particularly the Czech Republic. The first theme is privatization, which has significantly altered the relationship between government and the market in the areas of ownership rights and the rules of economic life. The second is the establishment of corporatist institutions, which occupy a unique position within civic sector organizations because government may pass some of its responsibilities on to them. The third is the appearance of corruption and mafias, socially pathological forms of 'regulation' that appear when government is incapable of formulating and enforcing regulatory functions that correspond to existing conditions. The final theme is the role of public policy in defining the role, method of implementation, and relationship between the market, government, and the civic sector.

II. PROBLEM AREAS

8. Privatization

Privatization is an end in itself. It is not necessary to connect it with anything else, because every other end is implicitly included in it. Liberal faith is its underpinning.

Tomáš Ježek (1993)

1. Introduction

The unprecedented process of rapid mass privatization in the Czech Republic and elsewhere in Central and Eastern Europe has been the subject of intense study,[1] and even more intense political debate.

Privatization, no matter how it is defined, has a deep impact on the regulatory functions of government, the market, and, to a certain extent, the civic sector. However, it is impossible to ignore the importance of the value systems within the framework of which privatization occurs, and, in turn, privatization's impact on those systems. (Mlčoch, in particular, has done a great deal of work on this topic in the Czech Republic). Privatization may be seen as an attempt to transfer the maximum amount of regulatory power from government to the market, from the public to the private sector. This shift is made possible by transferring legal ownership from the state to private entrepreneurs operating in the market. It is important to note, however, that if the recipient of former government property is a region, county, or non-profit organization the proper term to describe this process is denationalization, not privatization. It is also possible to call this process the decentralization of ownership rights in the public sector. However, in the post-1989 jargon widely used in political documents and ministry regulations such denationalization is often improperly defined as a form of privatization.

Before 1989 the Czechoslovak state owned 95 per cent of the means of production, more than any other socialist state. The private economic sector was almost nonexistent. Responsibility for the economy was in the hands of a clumsy centralized power and the State Planning Commission was its technical executive apparatus. Nevertheless, there were many informal horizontal and even tacit vertical 'non-aggression pacts' in the economic sphere which were necessary to sustain a functioning economy. The management of the lower portions of the hierarchy, that of enterprises, gradually emancipated itself from the powerful grasp of the central apparatus. Despite the fact that management formally controlled only leadership positions, as a result of informational asymmetry management gradually became the *de facto* owner of government property, at least to a certain degree.

This was the situation in Czechoslovakia when the political earthquake of 1989 hit. Proponents of the new regime and a significant majority of the Czech people agreed that a market economy should replace the centrally led and planned economy. One condition of a functioning market economy, however, is private ownership of the means of production, and the question inevitably arose concerning how that might best be brought about when almost everything formally belonged to the state. The solution chosen by Czechoslovakia and other Central and Eastern European countries to solve this problem was the gradual 'large-scale' privatization of national property.

2. The Form and Extent of the Transformation of Property Rights

Legal ownership was transferred in the following ways in the Czech Republic (Češka in Švejnar, 1993, 8f): (i) Restitution. Property was returned to its former owners or their legal heirs in the amount of approximately 150–200 billion Czech crowns (the exchange rate in the early 1990s was approximately 27 Czech crowns to 1 US dollar). Not all former owners had their property returned, however: the law laid down that only those whose property had been nationalized after the communist takeover in 1948 were eligible. Additional restrictions applied to property that had been taken from citizens' associations, churches, agricultural corporations, and emigrants. (ii) Return of government property to the counties. This applied to property appropriated after 1948, as well as available non-agricultural land and the government housing fund. The estimated value of this returned property was more than 350 billion crowns. (iii) Transformation of socialist corporations into private corporations and businesses. This involved property worth around 100–150 billion crowns. (iv) 'Small-scale' privatization. This involved the auctioning of approximately 22,000 stores, restaurants, and services, estimated to have a nominal value of 21 billion crowns. The final amount paid was, on average, almost half as much again, bringing the total to 29 billion crowns. (v) 'Large-scale' privatization. Stock in selected state companies was transferred to all adult Czech citizens who were interested in participating in this property transaction. Nearly 4,000 medium-sized and large companies were privatized, with a final value of approximately 1,200 billion crowns; 321 billion crowns' worth of property was distributed to citizens or to investment funds selected by citizens by means of voucher privatization—213 billion crowns' worth in the first round and 108 billion in the second. Remaining property was privatized by direct purchase, public auction, or public competition. Other changes in institutionalized forms of ownership were also implemented, including the conversion of state-owned enterprises to joint stock companies, and the incorporation of standardized norms into formerly state owned—now joint stock—companies (Ježek, 1993, 2).

The total nominal value of this transformed property was approximately 1,900 billion crowns, or almost 200,000 crowns per citizen.

3. Institutional Analysis of Privatization

In the Czech Republic a number of economists have focused exclusively on the impact of privatization on society and the economy. They have often complemented their own macroeconomic approach with the tools of institutional economics, whose theoretical apparatus allows for the detailed analysis of relationships in particular institutional environments.

New institutions were founded by the Government to carry out privatization and denationalization, including the Ministry for State Property and Privatization (abolished in 1996), the National Property Fund, and the Consolidation Bank. Traditional institutions such as the Ministry of Finance, the Ministry of Trade and Industry, and the Ministry of Health also participated in the privatization process. The Czech National Bank played a major role in controlling and privatizing the banking sector. By contrast, investment funds were established almost independently of the state and sought to control as much as possible of the property distributed to citizens by means of voucher privatization.

The process and results of voucher privatization were rated very highly by government economists. They highlighted the speed with which privatization had been carried out and its role in changing the structure of ownership, creating economic interest and establishing competition. They rejoiced in the country's apparent success in maintaining the stability and convertibility of the currency, low inflation, and a balanced budget, despite the rapid and massive changes that had occurred in ownership. They pointed to the boom in business activity and privatization's positive influence on the level of customer service.

Institutional economists and other specialists have been far more cautious in their evaluation, raising a number of significant criticisms. One important criticism is that the managers of former state-owned companies were able to take control of newly formed state joint stock companies within the framework of a system of completely liberalized prices which made any control by the National Property Fund impossible. These companies were free to do business with private companies that had been established by these same managers or persons closely connected to them, including family members. This made it possible to transfer finances from state joint stock companies to private enterprises, sometimes leading to the bankruptcy of the former and their subsequent purchase by the latter at very low prices.

Secondly, former members of such organizations as the State Planning Commission or managers of state-owned holding companies or trusts 'moved over' to newly established banks and investment funds, taking with them sensitive information about the financial situation of companies which they used for illegitimate personal gain in the developing capital and property markets.

Furthermore, although voucher privatization formally established private ownership, in terms of actual distribution a significant degree of state ownership still existed. This was true of a number of large companies and investment funds.

Among other criticisms, concern was expressed concerning the activities of the largest Czech banks—in which the state still had significant holdings—which created an ownership net upon which many business organizations, including smaller banks and companies both large and small, became dependent. Banks and affiliated investment funds attained enormous power by means of privatization within the framework of property legislation which was neither efficient nor transparent. Banks and investment funds controlled hundreds of their own portfolios, rendering individual shareholders powerless. Mlčoch (1996) refers to this structure as a "group oligopoly" which exercised considerable influence over the government and behaved as a monopoly in the banking sector.

Investment funds and banks, often in the dual role of owner and guarantor, have also failed effectively to exercise their ownership privileges *vis-à-vis* the management of large joint stock companies. Under threat of bankruptcy, or in direct collusion with management, they prolonged the necessary financial restructuring and provided resources to bankrupt companies in order to keep them going.

The activities of investment funds were not properly regulated by law either, and they had little regard for shareholders' rights. The same was true of small joint stock companies privatized through voucher privatization, particularly when powerful shareholders controlled the majority of stock.

The Czech capital market's lack of transparency and the difficulty of obtaining basic information about it has caused foreign investors in particular to become cautious. Many Czech investors used secret information, forestalled or manipulated the flow of information that should have been public, and furthered private aims by means of other illegitimate and immoral practices. Government control of the capital market was weak. It did not confront illegal practices even when, after years of hesitation, newly passed regulations empowered it to do so.

As a result of all these failings a number of the problems which had plagued Czechoslovakia towards the end of socialism survived after 1989. Products of quasi-state—now quasi-private—institutions were appropriated by private companies or persons, leaving the state—in other words, taxpayers, employees of bankrupt companies, and clients of bankrupt banks—to shoulder the economic risk. The Czech Republic had comprehensive "private ownership as far as the law is concerned, but with continuous 'core' state ownership and socialization of the negative economic results" (Mlčoch, 1997, 71). If privatization is improperly controlled by government only the profits are privatized while the losses are socialized.

Example:

A series of banks established after 1989 declared bankruptcy during the first years of economic reform. By the end of 1996 the total number of bankruptcies had reached twelve. Losses were estimated by the Czech National Bank at 40 billion crowns: independent specialists put them at hundreds of billions of crowns. The Government—and companies co-owned by the state—had shares in many of these banks, and government authorities kept their budget resources in them. These bankruptcies entailed losses of billions of crowns for shareholders and taxpayers, not to mention a collapse in confidence in the banking sector and the transformation process as a whole. To a significant extent these losses were borne by the Government or by banks in which the Government had a large holding. A major cause of these problems, besides inexperienced civil servants, was ideological prejudice, which found expression in such utterances as: "an enlightened government does not intervene in banking", and "the market can do everything". These attitudes led to a careless application of administrative regulations and control executed by the Czech National Bank and the National Property Fund in the banking sector. However, these losses were caused to a certain extent by conscious 'tunneling' which took place when 'loans' were offered to companies that had been founded by major bank shareholders with no expectation that they should be repaid.

---

4. The Role of Government and the Market in Transforming the Economy

A lack of transparency, together with the coalescence or even merging of government and market institutional structures, not only undermined the economy, but also threatened its potential for future development. Analysis of the privatization process in the Czech Republic during the period 1990–96 makes it possible to draw the following conclusions. A legal amendment defining the state as owner in the changed political and economic circumstances has still not been passed. In one sense, government has not completely renounced its role as the direct guarantor of economic functions. Although this role has changed enormously since 1989, the largest banks—which took over the regulatory functions of the abolished State Planning Commission—are still almost entirely state owned. On the other hand, government has not defined its role in areas where it would be particularly useful: for example, in formulating rules of competition for former state-owned companies. As a result, the Czech economy has remained inflexible in many respects.

The Government has yet to assume its role as an indirect regulator of the market activities of a range of economic actors in a satisfactory manner. Far from maximizing economic efficiency, the inadequately regulated market has instead promoted the improper—from the point of view of the public interest—transfer of profits.

Decision-making concerning privatization, as laid out in the relevant legislation, was not regarded as public. It was not subjected to normal administrative procedures and could not be investigated by an independent court. The process of privatizing state property was not institutionally transparent—opportunities for illegitimate personal gain were made available to persons with access to information or 'in the right place at the right time', often officials of the previous regime.

Ownership rights could be successfully claimed only with difficulty, which elevated the risk of illegal practices. We address this issue in more detail in chapter 10.

A significant portion of the economy was privatized only formally: "The restructuring of ownership relations meant a transition from quasi-ownership structures of formally state-owned property to quasi-private structures of ownership" (Mlčoch, 1994, 14).

The regulatory power of government did not allow it to enforce adequately even such laws as were available: "According to the police, there was no control of the transformation process, ownership relations, or the influence of foreign political and business forces in the economic sphere" (Cejp, 1995, 33).

These problems negatively affected the public's image of privatization, undermining the values of Czech society and the legitimacy of the new regime.

All of these factors constitute clear evidence of the state's failure as the authority representing the public interest in the privatization process.

In the Czech Republic the initiators of economic reform—including privatization—overestimated the capabilities of the market and private property, and underestimated the importance of regulation in the economy. "Looking at empirical studies based on data from particular companies, it seems that ownership is not a factor that systematically increases or decreases productivity. The most important elements seem to be an atmosphere of competition among companies, the imposition of strict financial limits, and the capacity to control and regulate management" (Švejnar, 1993, 1). Economic reformers also underestimated the ingrained behavior patterns of individuals and institutions, including the natural tendency to use 'tried and tested' models, thus perpetuating clientism in a formally new institutional environment.

Empirical evidence has been collected in the last few years which shows that the neo-liberal belief in the automatic self-regulation of the market was not borne out in practice during privatization. The Government significantly underestimated the need to create an adequate legal framework for the process of privatization, the establishment of appropriate capital market conditions, the exercise of property rights, government control of banks and other financial institutions, and conflicts of interest between public functions and private interest, let alone for repressing criminal activity (Jonáš in Ježek, 1993, 14).

Example:

Jiří Schlanger, chairman of the Labor Union of Medical and Social Workers in the Czech Republic, evaluated the results of Václav Klaus' neo-liberal government's privatization of medical institutions as follows: "The inappropriate application of market principles in a non-market environment, plus an inability to apply market mechanisms in the proper places, has borne sour fruit." The Prime Minister's belief that privatization was the best cure for the illnesses of the medical system led to harmful decisions in the transformation of medical care, a serious underestimation of the government's regulatory function, and inadequate approaches to existing problems.

A remedy was sought in partial technological changes in the regulation of the supply of and demand for medical care rather than in a global approach to changing regulations throughout the health care system. In *Proposal for a New System of Health Care* (Proposal, 1990b)—the only health care reform proposal accepted by the Government—the formation of a network of medical institutions was suggested which would guarantee standard medical care throughout the country. Instead of acting on this, however, the Government quickly privatized most medical institutions as if they were no different from industrial companies, factories, or shopping centers. "In the mixed economic system, the public sector was unable to react flexibly to private sector development, or to efficiently regulate the increasing cost of medical treatment by utilizing all necessary means" (Háva and Kružík, 1996, 13).

This approach to heath care reform is a clear case of trying to save money in the wrong place. Insufficient government involvement in health care and its inability to analyze independently the financial investments necessary to optimize payment for medical services or to improve price regulation of prescription drugs has had serious effects, including the loss of billions of crowns, not to mention considerable prestige. Because appropriate legislation for non-profit organizations—the most common institutional form of health care around the world—did not exist, the effort to privatize medical institutions rapidly was condemned to failure, resulting in chronic uncertainty on the part of management and employees about their future, including the form of new ownership relations.

Majone (1994) comes to the surprising conclusion that privatization requires even greater regulation than state-regulated economic activity. Although some would contest this view, it is clear that privatization represents a transition from direct to indirect regulation and so requires precise and strict external limitations if private initiatives are to be fruitful.

5. What Comes Next?

To some extent, privatization is an irreversible process. Despite all the weaknesses and implementation problems inherent in it, the effects of privatization are social facts. The Government, whose failures in this process we have attempted to illustrate in this chapter, should try to find the strength to correct some of the damage it has caused.

In short, the fundamental aim should be to reconstruct or reconstitute the regulatory function of government in places where its absence has clearly resulted in economic inefficiency or allowed individuals to profit at the public's expense. This is the least which the Government may 'get away with' because the new structure of ownership will not stabilize for at least five years. Another important step would be the detailed investigation of the criminal activity which was so central a feature of Czech privatization and punishment of the culprits. Only in this way may a functional and dynamic balance be struck between the market and government in terms of regulation and the exercise of ownership rights, thus—hopefully—renewing people's faith in both institutions. "Too often, the relationship between the private and public sectors is interpreted as a zero-sum game—that is, the increasing prosperity of the former may be attained only at the expense of the latter. However, the character of the modern state is such that the prosperity of both sectors is inseparably connected" (Moe, 1987, 453).

9. Corporatism

There is a certain range of policy areas for which institutions of group self-regulation may produce more socially adjusted and normatively acceptable results than either communal self-help, free trade, or *étatisme*.

Wolfgang Streeck and Philippe Schmitter (1995)

1. Introduction

Corporatism enables the civic sector and government to meet and co-operatively resolve many regulatory tasks. In the context of the development of Central and Eastern European countries since 1989 the degree and scope of corporatist institutions have become important issues as they will affect the form of these societies in future decades.

The terms 'corporatism' and 'corporatist institution' indicate specific relations of interdependency between government as a representative of the public interest on the one hand, and non-profit organizations as representatives of group interests on the other. In democratic societies with free market economies corporatist institutions help organize, balance, and modify group interests to correspond with public interests. In so doing the risk of unresolved and irreconcilable differences is reduced.

Government gives up part of its responsibility for monitoring and satisfying public interests, and, provided that the interests of corporatist organizations overlap with public interests, delegates its responsibility to them.

Example:
Professional chambers, such as the Czech Chambers of Physicians and Dentists (described in more detail later in the text).

Government can also participate in negotiations between non-profit organizations that represent different interests, so helping them to find a balanced compromise. In such negotiations government ensures that the public interest is not forgotten or abused.

> *Example:*
> The Council for Economic and Social Agreement—in short, tripartism (described in more detail below).

Government creates a legislative or consensus-based framework alongside specific rules that govern the operation of corporatist institutions. Its main function is to guarantee that non-profit organizations do not damage public interests or exceed the limits of their power while pursuing their own interests.

Corporatism in this sense is categorically different from that of fascist or communist states. In Mussolini's Italy, Hitler's Third Reich, and the Soviet bloc corporatist institutions were the obedient tools of the political leadership and a key element in the totalitarian power machine (on which they depended for survival) which stood against democracy. Not only are corporatist institutions as we understand them invulnerable to government abuse, but they prevent a disproportionate and potentially dangerous concentration of power at the center. Schmitter differentiates between corporatism in market economies and totalitarian regimes in terms of "social corporatism" and "government corporatism".

Corporatism as we understand it is characterized by the strategic interdependence of the participants. Government is dependent on the activities of non-profit organizations, which in turn rely on the proper functioning of government and other non-profit organizations. Their activities have a predictable positive or negative effect on the satisfaction of one another's interests, so they have a strong motivation to enter into relatively permanent mutual agreements. The necessity of frequently engaging in negotiations leads to voluntary mutual adaptation, so reducing the temptation to abuse short-term advantages that could lead to long-term losses for some or all parties.

Theoretically, corporatism may be interpreted as either the employment of privately organized interests to support public interests, or an abuse of public interests to support group or private interests. Although a realistic portrayal of the character of corporatism is provided by neither extreme, its role and function are the subject of many theoretical disputes among economists, political scientists, sociologists, and politicians. For neo-liberals, corporatist institutions are obstacles which deform and sometimes even hinder the operation of market forces, free contract negotiations, and the preservation of political freedom. They represent an unwarranted interference in the network of free market and civic relations by instituting group privileges obscured by a thin veil of higher public interests. In this way, according to neo-liberals, corporatist institutions lead to discrimination against people who are weak or poorly represented. Some neo-liberals go so far as to deny the existence of public interests at all: "In a market society . . . it is not necessary to hide individual interests behind the facade of higher goals. The only higher—the highest—goal is the recognition of one individual's interests over another's interests, which are then presented as higher interests" (Klaus, 1996, 260).

Consideration of the concept of organized interests and their relation to the common good has a long theoretical tradition. Durkheim and Tönnies studied this topic from a sociological point of view, Keynes from an economic one, and the papal encyclicals *Rerum Novarum* (1891) and *Quadragesimo Anno* (1931) dealt with its relationship to theology. The neo-corporatism of the 1970s and 1980s also developed a number of interesting theories and empirical generalizations, incorporating concepts from the political analysis of interest formation, organizational theory, management theory, and institutional economics. Moving away from an overestimation of corporatism as the cure for all ills related to the inherent imbalance of institutions in capitalist democracies, theoreticians of neo-corporatism have come to the realistic conclusion that its function is to serve as "a tendency, strategy, or partial structure in the mediation of interests in contemporary Western European societies" (Brokl, 1995, 9).

Central to theories of corporatism are corporatist institutions which inter-mediate between government, the civic sector, and the market. Many authors (including Lehmbruch and Schmitter, 1982; Streeck and Schmitter, 1985; and Uphoff, 1993) conclude that corporatist institutions have the potential—at least in developed Western democracies—to contribute to the regulation of the mutually adjustable and predictable activities of social players, both permanently and autonomously. The main principle of their interactions and allocations is the facilitation of institutional adaptation within a framework of negotiation which mediates the effective harmonization of interests and politics. It is negotiation "within and among a limited and fixed set of interest organizations that mutually recognize each other's status and entitlements, and are capable of reaching and implementing relatively stable compromises (pacts) in the pursuit of their interests. A corporatist order [consists of] interdependent complex organizations" (Streeck and Schmitter, 1985, 10). They add that "by deliberate mutual adjustment and repeated interaction, these comprehensive, monopolistically privileged actors avoid the temptation to exploit momentary advantages to the maximum and the pitfalls of landing in the worst possible solution. In short, they avoid the prisoner's dilemma through inter-organizational trust" (ibid., 13).[1]

Corporatism tends to emerge as a pragmatic political response to the dysfunctioning of democratic capitalism. Corporatism may be introduced from below, if civic sector institutions convince government that they should be utilized as means of responding to a segment of public interest that is better satisfied when government promotes specific civic-sector interests. The signal may also come from above, for example, during a period of crisis when politicians see that such an institution could support and successfully moderate the direct participation of interest groups in the functioning of government. "Institutions are only able to change gradually and marginally until the institutional context enables new negotiations and compromise among 'actors'. Political institutions, both formal and informal, may provide the framework for such negotiations. The problem is that a framework for resolving problems and conflicts does not exist until these institutions are created. With that comes the opportunity for the formation of coalitions with violent goals, which the actors perceive to be the only possible method of changing the institutional framework" (Mlčoch, 1997, 95).

A particularly important element in the relationship between government and non-profit organizations is the former's delegation to the latter of some degree of direct regulatory competence in a defined area of public policy. At the same time, in a corporatist agreement government sets procedural rules which bind the organization and maintains indirect control over its activities in order to ensure that it acts responsibly in pursuing specific public interests. The transition from direct to indirect regulation does not necessarily mean that government's negotiating position becomes weaker. On the contrary, government can become more effective because its bureaucrats are no longer burdened with aspects of the regulated activities that they do not completely understand and have more time to dedicate to the key parameters of decision-making in pursuing public interests.

One important mechanism that encourages interest-representing organizations to satisfy the public interest responsibly is the threat of direct government intervention. Government monitors and influences the activities of established corporatist institutions. Without that power it would be possible for an interest organization to colonize and manipulate a given segment of public interests for the benefit of its members. "It is only to the extent that the state—by a combination of procedural, instead of substantive, regulation with a credible threat of direct intervention—can hold private governments at least partially accountable to the public that the associative–corporatist mode of social order can become a legitimate alternative to communitarianism, *étatisme* and market liberalism" (Streeck and Schmitter, 1985, 26).

One advantage of corporatism is that elements of policy creation and implementation overlap in the activities of corporatist institutions. This differs from government which may face an 'implementation deficit', that is, an inability to realize policy. It is common for government to accept a policy, but to have insufficient sources to be able to implement it effectively. In corporatist arrangements, however, policies are often accepted after a series of difficult negotiations. Once they are completed, policies have a better chance of being accepted by all affected parties because their legitimacy has increased in the eyes of both professionals and clients during the negotiation process.

In the remainder of this chapter we shall focus on two typical corporatist institutions, professional chambers and tripartism, as they have existed in the Czech Republic since 1989. On the basis of these examples the chapter concludes with an attempt to illustrate the relationship between corporatism and democracy.

2. Example: Professional Chambers

Professional chambers are a typical form of corporatist institution. As examples we will look at the activities of the Chambers of Medicine and Dentistry since 1989. In the Czech Republic chambers are now mandated to develop and control the professional and ethical codes of conduct of their professions—a task which was mistakenly placed in the hands of government institutions during the communist era. Looking at the functioning of these chambers in previous years it is clear that their real activities were rather different. Both chambers strongly asserted the economic interests of their members, sometimes to the detriment of the public interest, particularly in relation to various health care program and reform documents. The Ministry of Health, as a representative of government, has failed to protect the public interest because it has been unable to draft proposals and realize health care reform successfully. Rather than viable cooperation between government and civic sector institutions there have been continuous disputes, aimless maneuvering, and a division of spheres of interest. In addition, the center has not been able to moderate a dialogue between different interest groups to benefit the sector as a whole—or patients.

Example:

After Luděk Rubáš was appointed Minister of Health in 1993 a proposal was made that he should introduce 'health multipartism' in the form of body that could act as a permanent platform for dialogue among interest group representatives (chambers, health care trade unions, and the Union of Invalids), institutions (insurance companies, hospital unions, and doctors), and the Ministry. In response, the 'Consultation Committee for Health Policy' was created. After some initial enthusiasm, however, Rubáš lost interest in this body. Meetings stopped and the committee did nothing to mediate the sharp conflicts of opinion which separated the main actors in health care policy-making. As a final consequence, less than two years later a conflict between health care interest groups and the public administration escalated into a series of strikes by doctors and other health care personnel. One of the official reasons for dismissing Rubáš as Minister of Health in 1995 was his inability to find common ground with the health care profession.

During these years the attitudes exhibited by both chambers were formed mostly in response to the failure to reform the Czech health care system. The salaries of doctors and dentists, which during communism had been kept very low, had been overlooked for an unacceptable period of time after 1989. Nobody should have been surprised that doctors and dentists forgot the original mission of their chambers when comparing the incomparable—their salaries and status in the Czech Republic in relation to those of their colleagues in neighboring Germany, for example—and began to use these institutions to struggle systematically to improve their social and economic status. One positive outcome was that, after several years and many painful experiences, they realized they could not count on bureaucrats in the Ministry to provide elaborated or consistent reform concepts and started to draft reform proposals themselves to overcome the organizational, legislative, fiscal, and moral crisis of the Czech health care system.

Some argue that because chambers sometimes exceed their powers their activities should be limited and their responsibilities transferred to public bodies. This is one possible 'choice of society', embodying a preference for a 'pure' model of representative democracy. It is doubtful that this would be the best solution, however. Chambers are undoubtedly suffering from growing pains that require immediate attention; on the other hand, limiting their development would be like throwing out the baby with the bath water. Professional chambers, like other corporatist institutions in the Czech Republic, have tradition, cultural support, and an opportunity for functional and publicly beneficial development. What they need is a strong and reliable partner—a competent government that is aware of its responsibility for providing health care to citizens.

3. Example: Tripartism

Tripartism is institutionalized negotiation between representatives of the so-called 'social partners': government, unions, and employers. Participants agree to respect joint decisions concerning economic and social policy. Specifically, representatives deal with employment issues, wage policy, and working conditions, and agree to implement the approved policies within their jurisdictions.

3.1 Experiences with Tripartism after the Second World War

There is a variety of approaches to the conduct of social dialogue between government, labor, and business.[2] This is especially true in developed capitalist countries, which may serve to inspire Central and Eastern European Countries as they search for their own solutions. In the West, two approaches have been identified: (i) complete functional tripartism, and (ii) an institutionalized dialogue limited to government and business. In a number of other countries there is no tripartism at all.

In countries with fully functioning tripartism, not only government, but unions and employers as well have developed and nationally centralized institutional foundations. There is generally no limit to the scope of topics discussed for the purpose of reaching a mutually acceptable compromise between representatives of the main interest groups; put simply, any matter that affects the participants may be brought up for discussion. In this scenario, social policy is a natural topic to be considered in discussions about government economic policy. "At a time of slow growth and rising aspirations, labor, interested in wages and social security, is forced to take account of inflation, productivity, and the need for investment; employers, interested in profit, productivity and investment, are forced to take account of social policy; both labor and management are forced to take account of government concern with economic performance, tax revenues, and the balance of payments" (Wilensky and Turner, 1987, 11). The Netherlands, Austria and, to a certain extent, even Germany and Denmark belong in this category, although in the latter two countries negotiations are more decentralized and tied to individual sectors of the national economy. Another country in this group, Sweden, stresses the importance of direct negotiations between representatives of employers and employees.

Countries with institutionalized dialogue between government and employers do not invite the trade unions to participate—only representatives of industry, trade, agriculture, professional chambers, and government take part in negotiations. Discussions center around how to draft and mediate policy in various sectors, with the emphasis on their impact upon economic policy. Trade unions in these countries are usually weak or truncated, and unable to agree on a coordinated strategy to protect their members' interests. Social problems are generally addressed only when they have become too serious to overlook and require immediate intervention. Japan and France are typical representatives of this group.

In countries without tripartism, the social partners are not bound to respect the interests of any other group or procedural obstacles in pursuit of their own interests. This means that they often overlook or even flout the public interest or the interests of other political actors. The United States and Great Britain, the countries with the greatest traditions of economic liberalism, are the foremost members of this group.

Table 9.1 compares the successes of individual countries in the areas in which tripartism is most effective: unemployment policy, inflation, and economic growth.

Table 9.1 Comparison of the Socioeconomic Indicators of Eight Countries with Full, Partial, or No Tripartism (based on average data from 1950–84)

Country	Unemployment (%)	GDP growth (%)	Inflation (%)	Orientation Index*	Rank
Japan	1.8	6.7	5.2	-0.3	1
Germany	3.3	3.9	3.9	-3.3	2
Austria	2.3	3.9	5.4	-3.8	3
Netherlands	3.4	2.9	5.3	-5.8	4
Sweden	1.9	2.5	6.9	-6.3	5
France	3.5	3.5	7.2	-7.2	6
United States	5.9	2.2	4.2	-7.9	7
Great Britain	3.9	2.0	7.3	-9.2	8

Source: Wilensky and Turner (1987) and the author's own calculations.

* The Orientation Index is the difference between average annual GDP growth and the sum of average annual unemployment and inflation.

As Table 9.1 illustrates, countries with full or partial tripartism were able to maintain lower unemployment and higher GDP than countries without tripartism. Only the United States succeeded in maintaining the same level of inflation as countries with full tripartism. On the whole, countries with full tripartism, together with Japan and France with partial tripartism, managed to cope with economic and social problems better than the United States and Great Britain which implemented a liberal model without institutionally mediated negotiations involving the social partners. In the 1990s the liberal model has proved itself in one respect, however: the countries adhering to this approach have consistently maintained lower levels of unemployment than countries with full tripartism.

Economic indicators did not develop favorably at the expense of social expenditure in countries with full tripartism, or in France with its partial tripartism. On the contrary, these countries were generally more generous with social benefits than those without tripartism. On average, between 1950 and 1974 the share of social expenditure in GDP in these countries was between 18 and 20 per cent, while it was about 13 per cent in Great Britain and 9 per cent in the United States. Japan spent less than 6 per cent of its GDP on social benefits, less in relative terms than any of the other countries with which we are concerned. Credit for its economic success during the period in question may be attributed mainly to the Japanese government's industrial policy and to cultural factors.

The main differences between the effects of implementing the three models described above may be summarized as follows: Countries with fully fledged tripartite institutions are best able to coordinate their economic and social policies. They are able to reach agreement on how expected expenditure and profits will be divided among social groups. Countries with institutionalized dialogue between government and employers are able to propose and implement appropriate economic and wage policies. However, they implement active employment and social policies only with some delay, if at all. Policy-making is reactionary and deals with problems only after they appear rather than attempting to anticipate them and to prepare solutions ahead of time. Countries without tripartism do not have institutions that are able to develop long-term policy concepts and simultaneously provide sufficient support to the affected parties. This results in an inconsistent fragmentation of individual policies because parties attempt to maximize their own profits, with no respect for the impact of a given policy on other social actors or on the country as a whole.

Comparisons of the development of selected capitalist countries have brought to light a number of strengths which characterize institutional arrangements involving full tripartism. (i) Communication. Established paths of communication and influence connect the social actors, facilitating mutually satisfactory agreements in a rapidly changing economic and social environment. Effective communication becomes a requirement for policy implementation. (ii) Specialization. Specialists are able to enter the process of negotiation and policy formation more easily. This expertise increases the likelihood that rational solutions will be approved, as well as the probability that social partners will agree that these solutions are appropriate. (iii) Harmonization of interests. The social partners are aware of the interrelationships and interdependencies of individual policies and measures in both the economic and the social sphere. This reduces the risk that approved policies will be partial, unbalanced, a threat to social peace, or otherwise economically or socially detrimental. (iv) Subsidiarity. Decision-makers are closer to the people directly affected by decisions and policies, which means that there is a better chance they will understand their problems and needs. As a result, these problems and needs may be considered during the processes of negotiation, decision-making, and subsequent implementation of policy.

3.2 Tripartism in the Czech Republic

The Czech people seem increasingly to have forgotten that economic and social policy, wages, and employment issues used to be decided by the State Planning Office.[3] Bureaucrats met, compared notes, and, when the number of workers required by individual enterprises exceeded the total work force in the economy, they did not argue or 'plan' for a larger work force. Instead, their attitude was 'the enterprises will manage somehow'. Wages rose more slowly than economic productivity—the economy stagnated, and wages and inflation increased. Nevertheless, the trade unions concerned themselves with recreational activities and the Government implemented the latest five-year plan approved at the congress of the Czechoslovak Communist Party.

Democracy has complicated everything. It has raised questions about what the optimal forms of dialogue and decision-making are—and who should participate in them.

The Council for Economic and Social Agreement is, understandably and correctly, most frequently considered in this context. The institution was established by the former Czechoslovak Federation in October 1990 and adopted by the Czech and Slovak republics some weeks later. It was a voluntary agreement involving the three social partners: government, trade unions, and employers. Tripartism was initiated by the Czechoslovak government and the Federal Ministry of Labor and Social Affairs, many members of the Civic Forum political movement taking their inspiration from the social democratic examples of Austria and Germany.

Since then, tripartism has functioned on the basis of the voluntary agreement of all participants. Neither its existence nor its relation to the Parliament have been formally codified in law, however.

The mandate of the Council for Economic and Social Agreement—until it was fundamentally revised in 1995—was to comment on all issues related to economic and social policy, particularly unemployment, living standards, and social and working conditions. It negotiated the contents of bills, drafts of laws, and regulations, and approved proposals for General Agreements each year. These agreements specified the obligations of individual partners concerning employment policy, wages, and social policy—basically, the progress of social reform.

After the elections in 1992 and a change of government a new vision of the future of tripartism in the Czech Republic was formulated and put forward in the fall of 1993. It reasoned that tripartism should function differently during the period of economic and social transformation and after its completion. During the transformation period, tripartism was necessary to keep the peace among the social partners; after transformation, however, tripartism should take the form of a body which advises and consults employees' and employers' representatives, while the role of government should be reduced to one of observation and the giving of advice. This proposal was not well received by the trade unions which insisted that the role of tripartism should not be defined too precisely. Another government proposal was to limit tripartite negotiations to wages, labor law, security, and health protection in the workplace. The unions insisted that the tripartite institution should have the right to comment on all important aspects of social policy and social laws.

The weakness of the trade unions became obvious in 1994 when the Parliament discussed social security legislation and new labor codes. The trade unions were opposed to proposals to eliminate employers' social insurance contributions for workers, to allow women to work night shifts, and to give employers the right to make temporary employees redundant without notice. Despite a protest demonstration organized by trade unions, the Parliament passed both bills as the Government had proposed them. It took the trade unions several years and many rounds of intensive negotiation within the tripartite institution to have wage regulations terminated.

Towards the end of 1994 the Government decided not to participate in tripartite negotiations in protest against the trade unions' threat to strike if their demands for the introduction of various legislative provisions and basic retirement insurance were not met.

The social partners finally succeeded in reaching a consensus in the spring of 1995, after a pause of several months and a national meeting of trade unions which supported the Czech Chamber of Trade Unions' dissent from government drafts of social laws. The tripartite institution was henceforth to be called the Council for Social Dialogue in the Czech Republic (this name was later changed to the Council for Dialogue of Social Partners) and was to negotiate issues related to labor law, labor relations, collective bargaining, employment, wages, salaries, job security, and social issues. Once again, the extent of the social issues to be considered was an area of conflict, especially between the trade unions and the Government.

The new Council functioned as a forum for ongoing dialogue about various aspects of social policy, particularly wage policy, price development, and social benefits. The employers succeeded in decreasing the taxable-income base of self-employed entrepreneurs. The trade unions managed to improve working conditions and health protection, and implement employment policy provisions geared to supporting regions threatened by long-term unemployment. However, after the parliamentary elections in 1992 tripartism was characterized by constant tension and ever increasing difficulties in maintaining a balance between the corporatist character of the institution and the neo-liberal Government.

Example:
Comparison of the contents of the annual General Agreements reached between 1991 and 1994 shows that their formulation became increasingly vague and they contained fewer concrete resolutions, particularly on the government side. Between 1995 and 1997 no General Agreements were signed at all due to irreconcilable differences between government and trade union representatives on various aspects of social policy, including the minimum wage and other important issues.

Nevertheless, for a number of different reasons all the partners desire to maintain social peace. "Government has deliberately refrained from attacking the corporatist, organized system of collective bargaining at the central, branch, and company levels. In exchange, government expects trade unions to respect the structure of tripartism, not to mobilize their members, and to reconcile themselves to their inferior position in negotiations on the basic issues of wage and social policies" (Orenstein, 1994, 2).

3.3 The Fate of Tripartism in the Czech Republic

It is well known that institutional structures influence politics, but in the Czech Republic public policy is currently in a position to influence the design of institutional structures fundamentally. The fate of tripartism is thus not exclusively an academic question or the business of politicians, but an issue whose resolution will have a considerable impact on everyone.

International comparisons unambiguously favor the preservation and development of fully fledged, functional, and competent tripartism involving three equal and open partners. A number of specific features of Czech political culture, characterized by attempts to prevent direct political confrontation and reach agreement through compromise, support this solution. The Czech Republic is fortunate that, after the collapse of communism, umbrella associations of trade unions were established to represent the interests of employees and employers at the central level which have become equal partners with government. Tripartism has contributed to preserving social peace and allowed the Czech Republic to be relatively successful in overcoming a difficult and socially risky period—the first steps in political and economic transformation.

The attitude of the Klaus government in the period 1992–97 was, however, quite different. The Government tried to sideline tripartism by dressing it up in the guise of non-binding negotiations between employees and employers and portraying itself as arbiter and observer. If it had succeeded, employees and employers would have been forced to watch helplessly as the Government proposed and passed bills with which they were expected to comply. Their only other alternative would have been to utilize confrontational methods such as strikes and other forms of civil disobedience to express their discontent. This truncation of tripartism would not have been worthwhile in the long term.

Tripartism does not function in this way anywhere in the world. Swedish tripartism has perhaps the lowest level of government participation, but there is no danger that one-sided proposals would be adopted regardless of the opinions of the other interested partners because of Sweden's political and cultural traditions of resolving political conflict through negotiation.

4. Democracy with Corporatist Elements: Yes or No?

Once established, corporatist institutions become part of a country's political system.[4] What are the specific functions of corporatism, and what are its strengths and shortcomings in establishing democratic structures and cultivating democratic consciousness and behavior in citizens? It is difficult to answer these questions without first answering another, more general question concerning the position and mission of policy in public life. Karel Čapek (1993) thought that politics were intended not only for political parties, but also for promoting public well-being. In other words, policy is not only the struggle to acquire and retain power, but also to present, recognize, and satisfy differentiated public interests. It is quite impossible to separate policy from the process in which it acts as a catalyst or a vehicle of inhibition.

Example:
In the second half of the nineteenth century Czech society was not yet strong enough to be fully politically emancipated from the Austro-Hungarian Empire. However, the flourishing Czech education system, culture, Sokol (an athletic organization that cultivated both the bodies and the souls of its members), and communal politics had an indisputably political dimension. They prepared the nation for the reclamation of political power—and *via facti* had already done so. After this experience, enlightened political leaders became aware of how important it was for the nation to gain, little by little, control over its own public affairs.

This remains valid, even more so than at the end of the last century or during the period of Masaryk's and Čapek's Czechoslovakia, in the years 1918 to 1938. The world is now incomparably more complex. The processes of forming and implementing differentiated interests are more colorful and closely connected with satisfying a range of partial interests. These interests are often difficult for someone without direct experience, be it a professional, layman, donor of a service or its recipient, to understand. In this situation, corporatist institutions function as mediators of information. By negotiating and implementing decisions they create additional channels of communication between citizens, interest groups, professionals, and political representatives.

When Václav Havel, President of the Czech Republic, refers to corporatism as apolitical politics it should be understood as literary exaggeration. However different it is from traditional power politics, it is oriented towards solving problems that affect citizens and their communities.

Two theoretical—and to some extent practical—alternatives face the Czech Republic. One is the model of 'pure' representative democracy; the second is representative democracy together with corporatist institutions. How do they differ? The 'pure' model of representative democracy, preferred by political and economic liberals and neo-liberalism, is founded solely on the concept of a set of individuals who are equal before the law. Bělohradský's thesis that "political decision-making is legitimate only if it is limited to enforcing basic laws, i.e., regulations binding for everyone" (Bělohradský, 1996, 6) forms the core of this way of thinking.

Corporatist democracy applies elements of both corporatist institutions and representative democracy, that is, the ability of citizens to express their interests and political preferences through elections. Unlike 'pure' representative democracy this model includes institutional mechanisms for presenting and enforcing the differentiated interests of various social groups and for their harmonization with public interests. These mechanisms fill the gap that can open up between individuals and the center of political power, but government influences their establishment, determines what role they are to play, and controls their functioning.

While considering which model of democracy is most suitable for the Czech Republic both historical traditions and the character of contemporary society should be considered.

For centuries the Czech lands of Bohemia and Moravia have been part of the Central European Christian cultural region, coexisting with neighboring Austria and Germany. Austria and Germany are corporatist democracies and delegation of a portion of government responsibilities to non-governmental institutions was a part of the Czech lands' history from the period of Enlightenment in the Austro-Hungarian Empire through the Munich Treaty in 1938, and then again, although in truncated form, from 1945 to 1948. The fact that the nation's historical memory is stronger than the forty-year uniformity of the communist regime became evident after 1989. Since then, both spontaneously and by conscious political choice, many mediating institutions of a corporatist type have been established.

Contemporary societies, including the Czech Republic, are much more complex than the early capitalist societies that give birth to liberalism two centuries ago. The networks of social cooperation and commitment, group and institutional links, interests and responsibilities are too dense to be mediated solely by institutions of representative democracy. Decision-making based on the principle of majority rule sometimes conflicts with decision-making based on expert analysis or respect for minority rights. Professional careers are as variable as lifestyles. In the information age citizens have access to almost as much information as their political leaders.

Political decision-making nowadays is a complicated process dependent on diverse individual and group interests that often conflict with each other and with legitimate public interests. Corporatist institutions pursue long-term interests that are not inhibited by four-year election cycles. They also control the level of professionalism of government bureaucrats when they resolve specific problems of public life, and occupy space that may be filled with oligarchies of the elected political elite in a representative democracy. One weakness of representative democracy is the danger that disproportionately centralized power may emerge in the absence of sufficient checks and balances, or as a result of the suppression of spontaneous citizen initiatives that attempt to influence the goals and tools of high-level politics. In this way, politics may fail to address the authentic problems people face in their everyday lives.

The control of politicians made possible by democratic elections is one of civilization's greatest achievements. But how effective is this control? In many cases it is insufficient to create barriers against abuses of power, since they may be easily overcome by economic power, and action may be seriously delayed. If political power is not balanced by other control mechanisms it can easily be diverted away from the interests of the people it represents, its principal clients—citizens.

Democracies with corporatist elements have flaws as well. There is greater institutional complexity, which can result in 'clumsiness' in situations requiring immediate intervention. (However, is this not a weakness of all democracies?) They are more dependent on personal responsibility, on the morality of representatives and members of corporatist institutions, and on the level of political culture in a given society. It is possible to question whether post-communist civil societies are morally prepared to shoulder a larger portion of responsibility for public affairs through the agency of corporatist institutions.

However, without trials there are no errors. Implementing corporatism in Central and Eastern Europe in the current climate gives empowered citizens additional opportunities to participate in formulating and executing political power, and in this way gives the entire political system more legitimacy. The importance of this cannot be underestimated, given that legitimacy is currently diminishing in all democratic, capitalist countries. Corporatist democracy encourages participation in establishing, implementing, and controlling policy. It raises public awareness of the necessity and importance of participation, and in doing so increases the trustworthiness of the entire democratic political system in the eyes of the public.

One final question remains: Is the enforcement of partial interests in democracy legitimate? The answer must be 'yes', if decision-making based on the rule of law is part of the democratic process. A corporatist arrangement becomes synonymous with narrow-mindedness and non-transparency only if its political role is not clearly defined and associated activities are not subject to regular public control. In any case, politics as rent-seeking is generated under democratic conditions not only by corporatist elements, but also by institutions of representative democracy, including political parties.

Corporatist institutions in the Czech Republic were damaged by the authoritarian regime. It is impossible to re-establish them quickly and from above, in contrast with the institutions of representative democracy. Favorable institutional and economic conditions that will encourage them to flourish must be created, or these still fragile institutions will not survive. This is why it is extremely important that Czech society, and perhaps other postcommunist societies that were forced to maintain an unnatural uniformity during communism, should be given the opportunity to revive traditional corporatist structures. Without them, these societies will be incomplete, partial, and alienated—in their monotony and in their citizens' lack of faith in their ability to influence public affairs—and they would revert to the conditions of the previous regime in all too many respects.

10. Corruption and the Mafia

1. Introduction

Socially pathological forms of regulation come into play when the power of the market is not effectively restrained. The means of such restraint generally include: the ethical reservations of actors themselves; an elaborate legal framework that prohibits activities in political and economic life that conflict with accepted standards of behavior; and strict enforcement of law by the state and its specialized institutions

Socially pathological forms of regulation destroy the moral foundations of society and lead to a whole range of injustices. In this way they endanger a country's political legitimacy and stability, as well as its economic prosperity. From an analytical point of view the fact that these phenomena can be perceived as socially pathological is not of primary importance. Rather, they are significant because, like the market, government, and the civic sector, they regulate the activities of individuals and legal entities.

While corporatist institutions attempt to optimize relations between public and group interests by way of complex and time consuming interactions, socially pathological forms of regulation live off public interests, or tame and subordinate them to private or group interests.

This chapter explores two social regulators that systematically and extensively deform the effective regulatory power of the market, government, and the civic sector to a degree that is unacceptable in a democratic state aspiring to support a civil society: (i) corruption and (ii) organized crime or 'the Mafia'.

Corruption is an abuse of the government apparatus for the purpose of obtaining personal or group advantages or direct benefits. Its principal tool is the bribing of civil servants, politicians, or political parties. The Mafia operates in areas where extraordinary profit, usually from illegal business activities, can be expected. Its typical sphere of activity is organized crime against property; if necessary, however, it does not hesitate to commit violent crime as well. Corruption and the Mafia are actually two distinct phenomena, although they sometimes overlap. When convenient, the Mafia uses the corruption of civil servants or politicians in the same way as entrepreneurs operating in other sectors of the economy.

We have chosen to discuss these dangerous forms of socially pathological regulation because they provide the most vivid illustration of what can happen when political, business, and financial interests clash. There are numerous other examples of this as well, including: the exploitation of personal privileges by civil servants; reciprocal awards of privileges; governmental appointments and decision-making based on biased interests; and the abuse of insider information regarding public decisions for private gain. In extreme cases, these phenomena can lead to total corruption of the government apparatus or to its direct colonization by the Mafia.

2. Corruption Connecting Government and the Market

Corruption is a method of obtaining unauthorized or undeserved advantages in exchange for payment or other services in the form of a bribe. Although it may occur in the private sector, this study focuses only on corruption that connects a private person or institution with a public person or institution, most commonly a politician or civil servant.

A specific market relation is created between the corrupting and the corrupted that cannot exist unless the corrupted person is influential in the government bureaucracy or politics, and prepared to abuse this status in exchange for a bribe. If this occurs, both the individual's character and government fail. Government fails because it is unable to ensure the equality of all citizens before the law—if one person or organization is unlawfully privileged, either another will be prevented from receiving a given public good, or the loss will be diluted among a greater number and the result will decrease the potential benefits of society as a whole.

As a society's morals and the control mechanisms inside and outside public administration are progressively weakened, corruption becomes more widespread. Evidence to support this hypothesis comes from two documents published in the last few years which prove that corruption undermines the national economy, international trade, and political stability of contemporary societies.

The Organization for Economic Cooperation and Development (OECD) published a report in 1994 which named corruption as one of the most serious problems facing contemporary societies. The report concludes with the recommendation that governments should do all they can to fight corruption at the national level.

In 1996 the Chamber of International Trade in Paris approved a series of recommendations for its members in their struggle against corruption. It calls for the urgent ratification of codes of behavior for civil servants, employees, and especially top management that are designed to prevent the offer or acceptance of bribes and to ensure the transparent registration of business contributions to political groups. Moreover, national governments are encouraged to pass laws which strictly prohibit bribery and extortion and to abolish forms of tax deduction that can be used as bribes. The Chamber also exhorts governments to prepare regular public reports that measure the control of bureaucrats who are either directly or indirectly involved in business transactions. Business contracts should be made in harmony with international, national, and corporate ethical codes. Finally, all business transactions, without exception, should be transparent, well documented, and subject to independent audit.

It is difficult to estimate the scope of corruption: what finally becomes known to the public is only the tip of the iceberg. Institutional economists interpret these expenses as transaction costs connected with pursuing a given economic activity, and conclude that such costs become higher as the reliability of the government apparatus decreases. "Some distinguish between a low level of bribery, say up to five per cent of total costs, which merely strains a system, and a ruinous level of bribery, which adds 100 per cent or more to the other costs of conducting business" (Etzioni, 1995, 208).

3. Corruption within Politics and the Financing of Political Parties

The corruption of politicians and political parties is a special topic. Politicians, as potential or actual representatives of public administration, and political parties, as organizations that formulate and execute political power, are constantly exposed to the influence of business and industrial circles. Theoretically, the division of political power should correspond to the division of societal interests. In practice, considerably more is invested in politics by business than by trade unions, civic associations, or individual citizens. Corruption of politicians and political parties, together with the redirection of the political mediation of interests to provide unauthorized advantages for corrupting business institutions, becomes inevitable if a transparent means of financing political parties does not exist.

Business sponsorship of political parties regularly endangers the public interest. This form of fund-raising for political activities poses the threat of altering political decisions to favor the rich, for whom this type of 'investment' is very convenient—after all, it is the taxpayers who have to foot the bill.

Example:
Financial resources earmarked for lobbying in the American Congress in the early 1980s brought some businesses (for example, dairy companies and Chrysler) huge gains in the form of laws sanctioning tax exemptions or higher subsidies. "Despite the rapidly rising cost of politics, it is a dirt-cheap business" (Etzioni, 1995, 232).

What mechanisms exist to provide financial support to political parties; how are they connected with possible conflicts of public and private interests; and what do Czech citizens think about them? Research conducted by the public opinion research agency IVVM cast light on these issues.

The financing of political parties by means of membership fees takes place on the assumption that political parties assert the interests of their members and that members are willing to pay for this benefit. This form of financing was supported by 89 per cent of respondents in 1994 and by 93 per cent in 1996. However, because the operating costs of a party apparatus are so high, no party could survive solely on this basis.

Some political scientists believe that a clear solution to this problem would be to support party activities from the government budget; this would be the best way of preventing political parties from being controlled by strong economic lobbies. Czech political parties currently receive considerable subsidies from the taxpayer, the amount depending on their electoral success. Popular support for this solution, however, is minimal, with 20 per cent of respondents favoring it in 1994 and 23 per cent in 1996. Moreover, the rule that political parties must gain at least three per cent of the vote in order to receive government subsidies is problematic because it discriminates against political parties that 'rock the boat' and pursue necessary programmatic innovations in a political scene full of conflicting group interests.

The majority of those asked thought that political parties should be allowed to engage in business activities with 61 per cent support in 1994 and 63 per cent in 1996. However, it would be dangerous to mix profit maximization with political activities the purpose of which is to pursue the public interest: conflicts of interest are almost inevitable. The resulting institutional hybrid would make the financing of political party activities—already difficult to control—even less transparent. Despite these potential pitfalls, however, a recent amendment to the Czech law on political party financing, which took effect at the beginning of 1997, permits this. A higher percentage of people agree with the idea of financing parties from business and other donations, with 69 per cent in favor in 1994 and 65 per cent in 1996. However, donations from sponsors in particular may dangerously influence political parties to support the economic interests of the rich to the detriment of the less well-off. Strong private interests may then be preferred to public interests, making political power a slave to economic power.

Perhaps it would be worthwhile to initiate a campaign to explain to people, especially those who are not members of trade unions or other organizations, why the preservation of a reasonable level of government subsidies would be in their best interests. This could be initiated by a group of political parties—if they could reach a consensus. There is more than sufficient evidence to illustrate the negative social impact of the funding of political parties from illegal sources.

Czech President Václav Havel proposed the creation of a special fund for 'political culture' by means of which political parties would receive both government subsidies and earmarked donations from sponsors. "Such a system would ensure public transparency regarding the sources of party funds, and at the same time it could function as a professional tool to identify their trust-worthiness" (Havel, 1995, 8).

No political party in the Czech Republic supports this project, and we might well ask why. One possible answer is offered by the many sponsorship scandals that have besieged political parties recently, particularly Václav Klaus's Civil Democratic Party. When it became publicly known that the party had falsely registered the sources of a number of sponsor donations, it was accused, at first, of maintaining an illegal bank account abroad. Later on it became clear that the actual sponsors were the owners of a company that had been given a lucrative piece of the privatization pie. The final result of this scandal was that, at the end of 1997, Václav Klaus had to resign as Prime Minister of the Czech Republic.

Political parties can also be corrupted in well camouflaged ways that may not even be illegal. The British Conservative Party and the Czech Civil Democratic Party both maintain a tradition of organizing dinners with the Prime Minister for interested business people. Firms pay huge fees in order to increase their visibility with top government representatives, and all profits go into the party coffers. 'Visibility' of this kind inevitably has an influence on government decisions about access to information sources, power, and money, rendering public control mechanisms ineffective.

Example:

The Premier Club was inaugurated in London in November 1995 to organize evenings for business people and various ministers, with an entrance fee of 10,000 pounds per head—100,000 pounds guaranteed two dinners with the Prime Minister per year. At one such dinner the attention of the companies which had donated money to the Conservative Party was drawn to a legal loophole which made it possible for their political contributions to be declared as 'entertainment' expenses and deducted from their taxable income. The then shadow minister of foreign affairs, Robin Cook of the Labour Party, called this the most obvious example of corruption in the history of the Conservative Party, and added, "Businessmen can now buy access and influence—it is enough to pay the Conservative Party under the table".

---

4. The Mafia between Government and the Market

Although our concern with the Mafia is confined to its role in postcommunist Central and Eastern Europe, a few historical examples will serve to clarify its mode of operation. In his excellent monograph Gambetta (1993) attempts to explain the origin and functioning of the Mafia, delineating the specific conditions under which Mafia organizations first began to provide 'services' to their 'clients'. In analyzing the unique features of Mafia organizations, some authors focus on their use of violence to ensure obedience, while others concentrate on their willingness to remain silent and even to suffer violence when necessary. Gambetta, however, distinguishes Mafia organizations in terms of their position between government and the market in particular social environments.

Consider how the Mafia proper emerged in its original homeland, Sicily, or how the branch of the Mafia in Naples, the Camorra, was created. Some historians and political philosophers attribute Sicily's atmosphere of distrust, especially towards government and its institutions, to the rule of the Spanish branch of the Habsburgs and subsequent governments of the Bourbons and Austrian Habsburgs, who ruled the south of Italy from the sixteenth to the nineteenth century by 'dividing and conquering'. As a result of this policy public administration was dispersed and inconsistent, and therefore unable to enforce the rule of law, especially in more remote regions. This distrust and institutional weakness negatively affected the social and economic potential of the island.

Such was the situation in 1860 when Garibaldi was able to combine Sicily and Naples into one united Italian kingdom. This was intended to bring about the end of feudalism and the beginning of liberal state rule. However, political and economic liberalization was undertaken when the young government was still weak and unable to present itself as a legitimate guarantor of law and order in the eyes of the Sicilian population. Uncertainty and distrust prevailed and well organized 'security agencies' continued to wield power. These agencies had originally been used by landowners to protect their property in villages, and they later gained experience in cities as protection fraternities. Given the new circumstances, they had an unprecedented opportunity to become independent— in contemporary terminology we would say 'to privatize themselves'.

Thus in Sicily private security and protection of property were not ensured through state centralization and monopolization, as was the common practice in many other countries. Instead it remained in private hands. Even so, the Mafia did not exist throughout Sicily and southern Italy. Omnipresent distrust and a weak state were necessary but not sufficient conditions for its creation. The third important condition was the existence of economic and political conflicts—the struggle for power and property. This happened in parts of Italy in the nineteenth century when vast tracts of municipal and church land were sold to private owners, and a struggle ensued for control of the fast-growing wholesale markets in the cities. For the rest of the nineteenth century and the majority of the twentieth, the Church, which did not support liberal rule, remained a tacit ally of the Mafia, appreciating the symbolic alliance and concrete assistance in its fight with the state.

Gambetta emphasizes that Mafia activity can be compared with that of a firm which produces, supports, and sells protection, and often begins when government is unable to fully employ its power monopoly to intervene effectively when laws are violated. The second necessary condition for the emergence of the Mafia is a lack of mutual trust among market actors. Protection is necessary in such a situation, although it is an inadequate and expensive replacement for trust. The Mafia enters the market by offering to protect its clients—from an economic point of view, payment for such protection is a rational course of action. While some become victims of blackmail, others become 'loyal customers'. Although individuals or firms are forced to accept such protection, that does not make this protection worthless. The Mafia is a private entrepreneur. It specializes in the sale of protection and fills a vacuum that, for various reasons, has been left by the state. On the other hand, Mafia organizations can also artificially stimulate the need for protection. However, in places where the market functions without government and without mutual trust, such organizations offer protection that no one else could provide.

Sometimes government bans particular transactions or the trade of particular goods but is unable to enforce adherence to these laws, thus expanding the sphere in which the Mafia can operate. Particular market segments become unstable, endangered, and fragile, not only because government does not sanction them, but also because perpetrators are sent to court, for example, a drug dealer who has been cheated by his distributor. This occurred in the United States during prohibition in the 1920s and is currently the case in many countries with respect to drugs, organized prostitution, and trade in illegal currency or radioactive materials; similar embargoes are sometimes imposed on weapons. It is not an accident that Mafias deal in all of these goods and activities.

At other times, the interests of Mafia organizations and government can even correspond. When a Mafia organization operates effectively and no disputes occur between its various clans and branches, a semblance of order prevails and there are few direct threats to the public.

Examples:

The relatively low mortality from drug overdoses in Sicily is allegedly due to the fact that the Mafia maintains a high quality level in respect of the drugs which it distributes.

Experienced observers allege that the local Mafia was the only organization in Moscow or St. Petersburg that could manage food distribution at the beginning of the 1990s. The Government had no choice but to tolerate it. Finally, if a Mafia organization has reason to dispose of ordinary street criminals, it does not hesitate to help the police apprehend and punish them.

Just like any other business entity, the Mafia has particular resources at its disposal. They include: (i) Secret information. Through their own information networks Mafias systematically collect and process information about markets, clients and their behavior, the behavior of potential competitors, and the situation in government security organizations. This information is kept confidential, or is only selectively distributed. A prerequisite for becoming a member of the so-called Sicilian Mafia is 'omerta', the willingness to keep silent even under duress, that is, the threat of death or violence to oneself, family members, or other loved ones. (ii) Violence. Contrary to widespread opinion, Mafia organizations do not seek violence. Violent crimes create panic and are the focus of undesired attention, which damages the trade in protection. Violence is a tool used deliberately and only in situations where a different course of action would not lead to the desired outcome. Even so, violence is one of the Mafia's most important commodities for three reasons. First, dealing out punishment is sometimes necessary for a professed protector. Second, it is impossible to avoid violence in open clashes among Mafia 'families', because if no one is willing to compromise or give in, such conflicts cannot be solved in any other way— government can hardly intervene as a mediator. Finally, another advantage of violence is that it is relatively inexpensive. (iii) Reputation. Reputation can attract customers and deter potential competitors from entering the already saturated market in protection. Most importantly, a 'good' reputation is cheaper because it can function as part of the protection itself: a 'reputation' for strength may persist even when it is no longer substantiated, and enables some Mafia organizations to provide protection successfully, even though they would fail if it became necessary to take action. (iv) Marketing. Although in a slightly distorted form, marketing and public relations are important even for the Mafia. Although they can hardly use all available forms of advertisement Mafia organizations have developed their own methods, often promoting their services through action, for example, by helping people through difficult situations, returning stolen property, mediating in conflicts, or donating to charity.

Mafia organizations make agreements with corrupt politicians and civil servants: they provide financial support for election campaigns or political parties and expect, in exchange, that these politicians and civil servants will tolerate Mafia operations, provide important information about government activities, and initiate attractive tenders for projects financed by public funds. Mafia penetration of public administration poses a serious threat to democracy by paralyzing the only organized force capable of restraining Mafia growth.

Example:
The Italian government's inability to eradicate the Mafia from the 1950s through the 1980s may be explained by the fact that the Mafia was supported by top representatives of political parties, government, and business. The struggle against the Mafia could never be consistent because its allies operated within the very structures that were designed to destroy it. In the end, however, government was relatively successful in dealing with the situation, for two reasons: (i) at the beginning of the 1990s the influence of once powerful mafiosi with allies inside the government apparatus began to decrease, and (ii) the Mafia never managed to obtain complete control of the state. As Gambetta writes in his monograph the Italian state "breeds both rats and heroes" (Gambetta, 1993, 8).

---

5. The Mafia in Postcommunist Countries

"A persistent lack of trust, fueled by the dying embers of feudalism and combined with the rise of a sinister breed of protectors from the ashes of the *ancien régime*: these may go some way towards providing a general account of the origins of the Mafia" (Gambetta, 1993, 81). This statement was intended to explain the situation in southern Italy at the end of the last century, but in many ways it describes the present situation in Central and Eastern Europe. There are many structural similarities. Feudalism and socialism were similar in the sense that under feudalism there were a few large owners and under socialism—at least theoretically—there was one gargantuan owner. These owners monopolized power, thus ensuring their ownership.

New government bodies, stemming from the monolithic Soviet Union and its previous satellites, are currently fighting to preserve their legitimacy and are experiencing economic problems. They have inherited an administrative and repressive apparatus that is unreliable and prone to corruption. As a result of political and economic liberalization ownership rights are being transferred from government to private owners—but the new owners do not have the same power as their predecessor. A new division of economic and political power is being created. Trust is a scarce resource, enforceability of ownership rights is low, and transaction costs are increasing. "In such a situation, there is increasing societal demand to create private mechanisms to protect ownership rights and guarantee repayment of outstanding debts. This may lead to the socially undesirable solutions of private arbitrage, violence, and Mafia practices replacing legal enforcement" (Shleifer, 1994, cited in Mlčoch, 1994, 12).

How did Mafia activity emerge in Central and Eastern Europe? Soon after the suppression of the anti-Gorbachev coup in February 1992 Viktor Barannikov, chief of the Russian secret service, fired 33,200 of the 36,000 members of the KGB. Democratization released from the government secret service thousands of men and women with above average intelligence, no scruples, and skills that allowed them to obtain and protect secret information. They were left to profit from their skills and wide connections in other ways. The wide media networks of former communist regimes, their access to information, and their special skills were a considerable boon for newly formed Mafia organizations. The same may be said for the specialists of physical violence, including bodyguards. Many people who had worked in the communist repressive apparatus had become useless in the new regimes and were left to seek other ways—usually illegal—of utilizing their special 'qualifications' in the market. Increased mobility of people, goods, and capital among states created opportunities for the Mafia beyond the borders of individual nation states. All this created an ideal environment for Mafia activity. "Organized criminals have access to substantial wealth, perfect information, high technology and perfect organization. They always try to make contacts in the government apparatus and with business leaders . . . Organized crime ruins government and business structures, destroys successful business accomplishments and devastates morality" (Cejp, 1995, 4, 8).

Example:
'Legalizing' profits from criminal activities—money laundering—illustrates the impact of liberalizing the capital market when government administration does not take effective parallel measures to preclude illegal activity: "confronting police with the consequences of these activities is not the only means of struggle. Rather, precise and uncorrupted bank and tax officers, plus strong legislation, are able to block the capital and financial activities of international organized crime" (Gabal, 1994, 88–89).

Czech Mafia organizations have obtained something of a stranglehold on public administration. The Czech government has so far done little to rectify the situation. Only as late as 1995 were a few amendments or rewordings of laws accepted that to some extent dealt with the Mafia, related to the prevention of organized crime, money laundering, and the operation of private security services (Cejp, 1995, 25).

As recent developments in Italy show, the struggle of government and the civic sector against socially pathological forms of social regulation—including corruption and the Mafia—can make progress. Hopefully, at some time in the future it will be possible to say the same about Central and Eastern Europe. A necessary precondition of reducing corruption and Mafia activities is the recognition that these phenomena are dangerous and widespread. In other words, the public must be made aware of the scope and seriousness of corruption and the detrimental activities of organized crime. These major enemies of a free society must be combated with sufficient resources, allowing honest, capable, and well-equipped professionals to work against them effectively.

11. The Role of Public Policy

> It is true that every social system and every human construct is imperfect, but the fact that we have unveiled the imperfections of one regime should not be used to justify its opposite. This approach is one of the most frequent human errors. The main teaching for us from the previous years is that narrow self-interest is not a source of values that allows us to resolve the political problems confronting us today.
>
> *George Soros (1991)*

1. Introduction

The definition of the roles, functions, methods of implementation, and interrelationships between individual regulators of social life is one of the most important tasks of public policy. It is particularly crucial at turning points in history, such as the one Central and Eastern Europe is currently experiencing. The formation of democracy and a market economy—what is this other than radical interference with the well established order, changing the manner in which the roles of the market, government, and the civic sector are understood and practiced?

As we shall attempt to illustrate in this chapter, the way in which public policy mediates the functioning of the market, government, and the civic sector may significantly influence the character of their regulatory functions and interrelationships. Implementing one solution rather than another will significantly influence the 'choice of society', and in that way will have a long-term effect on living conditions.

Public policy cannot define and shape the social regulators on its own. By means of public policy it is possible to deal with a variety of day-to-day problems, mediating, negotiating, introducing, and eventually abandoning particular agendas. Reflected in all these activities is a vision of desirable goals, priorities, and aversions concerning possible regulatory tools and political actors representing partial or general, private, group or public interests. Policy may be used as a tool to ease relationships between the market, government, and the civic sector—or it may create disharmony.

Recent research on Czech public policy has analyzed its development in thirteen areas considered to be important for the Czech state and society:[1] (i) social reform; (ii) family policy; (iii) housing policy; (iv) education policy; (v) the fight against crime; (vi) privatizing health care; (vii) managing health insurance; (viii) reforming public health care; (ix) moving from conscript to voluntary military service; (x) human resource policy in the Czech army; (xi) advancement of selected non-profit organizations (especially the Czech Association for the Protection of Nature); (xii) development of the mass media; and (xiii) the formation of local elites.

We began with the supposition that the results of a comparison of development in these areas would allow us to characterize the nature of the changes and more general developmental tendencies since 1989. This supposition has proved to be correct. We examined the development of the market (especially in relation to privatization), the functioning of public administration, and the birth of the civic sector in the abovementioned areas. Findings from this research enabled us to interpret the nature and problems of the political process as a mediator of social regulation in the following thematic areas: strategic management in the public sector; the political priority given to development of the public sector; the coordination of the activities of a number of political actors, including interdepartmental cooperation; communication between government, the Parliament, and the public; opportunities for experts to influence the formation and implementation of public policy; and the relationship between power politics and merit-oriented policy-making.

In the remainder of this chapter we examine each of these thematic areas in detail. Each area is introduced by a brief description of its current situation. Illustrative examples follow, selected from research conducted on Czech public policy and from other studies.

2. Strategic Management in the Public Sector

Table 11.1 shows the Czech government's acceptance of binding policy documents in the last several years.

Table 11.1 Acceptance of Binding Political Documents, 1989–1996

Date of the last document's acceptance	Policy area
1990	Health care
1990	Education
1990	Social policy
1991	Housing
1994	Fight against crime
1995	Environment
Not approved	Voluntary service in the army
Not approved	Public health
Not approved	Family policy

Generally, it is clear that the period between November 1989 and the elections in 1992 was most productive in terms of creating conceptions, policies, and programs. The year 1990 was particularly fertile in this respect—although this does not necessarily imply that approved and accepted conceptions were later implemented.

A radical change took place after the Klaus Government came to power in 1992. There was a shift towards *ad hoc* administration and day-to-day management, concentrating on means rather than ends. This led to the paradoxical situation that former employees of the Institute of Forecasting of the Czechoslovak Academy of Sciences, who had prepared the foundations of reform prior to 1989, were prepared to abolish the Institute after they attained power. They denied the usefulness of long-term forecasting and strategic management for effective administration and long-term prosperity. Neo-liberal ideologists attempted to justify this approach in terms of their objections to 'social engineering'. Even policy conceptions that had been approved by the Government often collapsed due to insufficient resources or incompetent administration in the ministries. In other cases, conceptions were fragmented due to 'gung-ho' voluntarist decisions, motivated by a pragmatic understanding and ideologically colored perception of the 'needs of the day'.

Housing Policy

In June 1990 the Commission for Technological and Investment Development of the Czechoslovak Government prepared "The Conception of Government Housing Policy after 1990". This was never officially approved. After that the Czech Ministry of Economic Policy and Development put forward "The Government Housing Policy of the Czech Republic". This new housing policy framework was passed by the Czech Government in 1991. The same ministry created another document in 1992 called "Foundations and Components of Government Housing Policy in the Czech Republic". This document, however, was never passed. In 1993 the Czech Government considered these proposals and based conclusions on them which were passed down to the appropriate ministries. No comprehensive document on the issue of housing has been approved since then.

The fact that government hesitation in the area of housing policy was known to the public is documented in public opinion surveys. In response to the question of whether the Government had a clear, long-term solution to housing problems, 55 per cent thought that this was not true, and only 12 per cent held the opposite opinion (Valentová, 1995; Valentová in Purkrábek et al., 1996).

Moving towards a Voluntary Army

"In 1991 the decision was made to move from conscription to voluntary service in the army. Relevant documents explored and negotiated that process. All of these research and negotiation processes, however, took place only within the army and never reached the government level" (Sarvaš, 1995, 100). Both the political and the military leadership have taken a shortsighted approach to this issue, envisaging time-frames of only three to four years. All of the organizations concerned tend to favor practical results, which derives from their desire to register concrete achievements within the shortest possible period of time.

Education Policy

The first Czech government after the fall of communism required the Ministry of Education, Youth, and Sport to prepare a prognostic study on the prospects for developing a new education system by the end of January 1991, which was to be used to develop a proposal for such a system. This study was never completed. The government which came to power after the elections in June 1992 promised to develop a modern strategy for education and education policy. However, no such strategy was discussed between 1992 and 1996. At the same time, several radical steps were taken that had a dramatic impact on the education system. Structural reform, such as the creation of eight-year high schools and the reduction of the period of required school attendance, was followed by normative financial reform, general and public school curriculum reform, and administrative reform which gave the Ministry of Education, Youth, and Sport sole responsibility for education, with practically unlimited decision-making power (Kalous, 1996, 115–16, 199).

Only one resolution was accepted between 1989 and 1996: 157/90 (May 23, 1990) on the program of changes in the education system. This program was intended to assure a smooth transition period from 1990 until the beginning of academic year 1992–93, but it was never implemented due to a lack of funds. Even so, it was not repealed—and no one objected (Kalous, 1995).

Health Care

In 1990 three proposals on health care reform were put forward, including: "A Thesis on the Health Care Program", published in January 1990 (Teze, 1990); "A Proposal for Reforming Health Care", brought forward for public discussion in May 1990 (Proposal, 1990a); and "A Proposal for a New System of Health Care", accepted in December 1990 as Resolution 339/90 of the Czech government, as a starting point for further health care reform (Proposal, 1990b).

The new system assumed that the market, government, and the civic sector would play distinct roles in health care and contained a comprehensive overview of the aims, measures, and steps necessary to reform it. No materials have been approved by government since then. Political practice took the form of rushing to implement individual steps, taken out of context, and focused solely on questions of health insurance and the privatization of health care: "It is typical for politicians to utilize short-term approaches in attempts to find 'quick fixes' for problems. A series of changes has been implemented that grows from the simple principle of emphasizing citizens' individual responsibility for health care, or that seeks mechanisms to narrow the demand for health care services" (Háva and Kružík, 1996, 1–2).

Public Health

"The development of problem solving in public health is complicated by the current disgraceful state of health care. The fact that the twentieth variation of a proposal is being created is a signal that something is not working properly. The multiple attempts would not necessarily be tragic in and of themselves, if the variants followed one another and each improved on the main conception. However, anyone who has had the opportunity to become familiar with the proposals knows that no well conceived conception follows . . . Authors of the proposals act as if they do not know what they want, or what they should want" (Ticháček, 1995, 52).

Law and Order Policy

Evidently due to the severity of rising crime and its negative effect on the public "The Program of Social Crime Prevention" was debated by the Czech Government on August 14, 1993, and "The Conception and Program of Crime Prevention" was passed in the form of Resolutions 617 (November 3, 1993) and 341 (June 15, 1994) (Cejp, 1995, 19). These were based on narrow departmental foundations and were therefore inadequate. "The creation of a law and order policy, if it is intended to ensure citizens' stability in society and not only to impose penalties for punishable activities, cannot be relegated exclusively to the fields of security and justice" (Gabal, 1994, 95).

Social Policy

The Czech Government accepted "The Scenario of Social Reforms" in 1990. Since then, no other conception has been accepted, but instead political momentum has led to the acceptance of a number of major and minor laws related to social security.

Family Policy

In the latter part of 1989 a new, unofficial conception of family policy was prepared as an alternative to the previous policy (Alan et al., 1989). After 1989, however, family policy as an independent area was never explicitly defined, as a result of which no attempt was made to elaborate its strategy (Munková, 1996, 6).

The Environment

"Government Policy on the Environment" was accepted by the Government in 1995 ('Státní', 1995). Analysts note, however, that although it outlines the Government's intentions in this area, it proposes neither an implementation strategy nor a binding program—rather it forms the basis for creating a long-term binding program. Concrete steps, such as the allocation of specific responsibilities or the definition of evaluation methods, are simply missing.

In order to formulate a desirable vision of Czech society, the need for which has frequently been emphasized by President Václav Havel, it is necessary to have comprehensive strategic plans or long-term programs in the abovementioned areas. On the other hand, without an overall comprehensive vision it would be difficult to create plans or programs that do not conflict. The need to begin a systematic, strategic, and conceptual study of these matters in the Czech Republic is explored in detail in the final chapter, "The Choice of Society".

3. The Political Priority Given to Developing the Public Sector

Comparison of policy development in areas generally considered to be part of the public sector shows beyond a doubt that the public sector was 'put on the back burner' after 1989, especially during the first Klaus Government (1992–96). Government policy clearly prioritized economic reform. This may be attributed, among other things, to the following: the doctrinal priorities and limits of neo-liberalism in advocacy and practical policy-making; the low competence of public administration, which was not capable of understanding, accepting, or utilizing innovations generated by citizen initiatives in the post-revolution period—this was partly the result of delays in reforming public administration and the absence of a systematic examination of the ability of civil servants to deal with the problems they were expected to solve; economic limitations, due to the fall in GDP and government expenditure in real terms.

At this point it would be worth giving a brief description of the situation in a number of important areas.

Housing
The ability of the Ministry of the Economy of the Czech Republic to act as a guarantor of housing policy between 1992 and 1996 may be judged in terms of the level of importance given to that policy. Only one department—which consisted of approximately ten employees and did not include an economist until 1994—worked on this issue, and the Ministry's organizational structure did not even include an official head of the housing policy department. In the Czech Parliament there was no committee on housing. Had there been a head at the ministry or a parliamentary committee, more administrative and expert attention would have been focused on the issue (Valentová, 1995).

Defense
After the attention paid to defense in 1990 it fell by the wayside as an issue for the political parties, which focused mainly on economic issues (Sarvaš, 1995).

Law and Order
"There has been a deficit of political, legislative, and executive attention paid to the issue of law and order . . . Opportunities, power, means, and the position of the police in today's conditions are likely to be insufficient when compared with the development of the situation in law and order" (Gabal, 1994, 95–96).

Social Policy
Social policy reform was considered to be a lower political priority than reform of the economic and political systems (Potůček, 1995b, 18).

> *Education and Health Policy*
> Development of the education and health care systems held far less interest for the
> government than the progress of economic reforms (Kalous, 1995, 88; and Potůček, 1994a).

4. Coordinating the Activities of a Range of Political Actors—Interdepartmental Cooperation

It is a prime responsibility of public management to ensure that the activities of public institutions are harmonized. It is of particular importance for departments and ministries to be consistent in regulating the activities of people and institutions. This problem was not thoroughly addressed when the Czechoslovak Federation was divided in 1992. At that time, the very definition of competencies and responsibilities was a political hot potato. Everything was changing rapidly, including the make-up of central administration.

The importance of harmonizing activities becomes particularly apparent during the interdepartmental process of analyzing and criticizing drafts of legislation and amendments. It also manifests itself within the framework of special commissions—whose members represent bodies that will or may be affected by the policy in question—in their work on these drafts.

The government elected in 1992 worked on these issues with varying degrees of success. It produced concrete results in some areas, such as the fight against crime, and no visible effect in others, such as health care. Government's role was certainly undermined by the desire of its leader, Václav Klaus, to avoid creating commissions with open coordination functions (for example, the Government's approach towards implementing medium-term projects to renew and support public health described later in this chapter).

> *The Fight Against Crime*
> Three bodies with interdepartmental functions were created:
> (i) A national committee for crime prevention, established by the Ministry of the Interior on January 1, 1994. This committee was created to facilitate negotiations between representatives of the Ministry of the Interior, the Ministry of Education, Youth, and Sport, the Ministry of Foreign Affairs, the Ministry of Justice, the Ministry of Defense, and the State Attorney's Office. The creation of regional and local boards for crime prevention was also recommended, envisaged as coordinating bodies to monitor the activities of local agents and serve as links to the national committee. They were to be composed of employees of appropriate local administrative bodies and had the additional task of developing elements of citizen self-protection. Unfortunately, these commissions are virtually moribund at the local level (Cejp, 1995, 19, 20, 30).
> (ii) An interdepartmental group, based at the Ministry of the Interior, to analyze and issue residence permits to foreigners in the Czech Republic.
> (iii) An interdepartmental anti-drug commission, set up in June 1993 and originally at the Ministry of the Interior. Since 1995 it has been under the patronage of the Prime Minister's Office.

Housing
Between 1990 and 1996 the division of responsibility among various government bodies in respect of housing issues was not clear. "The Ministry of Economy is responsible for housing policy, but the actual decision-making is divided between it, the Ministry of Finance, the Ministry of Labor and Social Affairs, and the Ministry of Industry. Coordination and communication between the ministries, which occurs solely in the form of parallel consultations and personal contacts between civil servants, has proven to be insufficient" (Valentová, 1995, 20).

Promoting Health and Preventing Illness
The national health program, accepted on July 22, 1991 as Government Resolution 247/91, called for the establishment of a medium-term project to renew and support health care. The establishment of this project was passed and approved as Government Resolution 273/92 on April 15, 1992. On the basis of this resolution an interdepartmental commission for the promotion of health was to be established which would coordinate at the central level all actors whose activities were related to health issues. However, after 1992 the new government did not feel bound by this resolution. A National Committee on Health was not created until June 1994, and even then its role in coordinating the work of different departments was not clarified. Its members were health care professionals, primarily hygienists (Ticháček, 1995, 47).

5. Communication between Government, Parliament, and Public

One important issue of public policy is the amount of information that is passed between government, Parliament, and citizens. Do government and Parliament discover early enough what citizens think about problems and proposed solutions? Do citizens have opportunities ahead of time to become familiar with political decisions that could substantially affect their lives? In order to address this issue satisfactorily we examine several situations and the approaches of different parties, and then look at how communications might be improved.

The Czech public is unlikely to attempt to influence public affairs directly, particularly in political discussions. The principles of social reform "have not been the subject of wide public discussion. A majority of the population is not capable of predicting the results of individual accepted steps and the advantages or disadvantages of other possible variants" (Munková, 1996, 7).

Gabal (1994, 96) posits that citizens, citizens' groups, and citizens' initiatives put insubstantial pressure on government and on legislative, administrative, and local institutions in respect of the amount of attention, money, and effort they dedicate to the issues of crime, violence, and security. A content analysis of articles in journals related to the privatization of health care showed that discussion of this theme was basically a dialogue between ministry civil servants and health care professionals. Citizens did not join in the debate (although the Patients' Rights Defense Association has recently made itself known).

The administration has not reacted favorably towards citizens' initiatives. During the debate on education reform "the Ministry of Education proved incapable of utilizing the proliferation of materials prepared by the educational community. Over one thousand pages of conceptions and proposals were sent to this Ministry by independent initiatives and merely collected dust . . . Through the power of bureaucracy, the opinion of the first civil servant—the Minister of Education—was [the one] finally put forward" (Kalous, 1995, 81n). Pedagogical initiatives flow into a vacuum because no organization exists that is able to propagate the interests of education's primary clients—students and parents— effectively. "Central administration and ministries still have insufficient experience in partnerships with schools, teachers, students, parents, and local administration. Few ministries have reorganized themselves or their activities to support a partnership approach, rather maintaining the traditional method of imposing requirements and requiring their fulfillment" (Kalous, 1996, 125).

As for health care, several conceptions on improving public health and proposed wordings of public health laws were developed, although none were ultimately accepted. These conceptions and proposals came from the Ministry of Health and were officially difficult to access, even by impartial specialists (Ticháček, 1995, 50).

The Government's proposed law on state social support was first discussed when, during a debate of the parliamentary Committee on Health Care and Social Policy, its faults and applicability were called into question by members of the Government's own coalition parties. With that incentive, the Committee organized a one-day seminar on this issue, and only at this point did the press begin to take an interest in the make-up of the Government's proposed law.

Objective and undistorted information about crime and citizens' safety is unavailable. This is a fundamental prerequisite of any meaningful debate, not only on public security, but on the efficiency of public expenditure in this area (Gabal, 1994).

What could help to resolve these communication problems?

In the first place, effective mechanisms have not yet been developed that would facilitate the participation of social partners at the central level—including representatives of the relevant branches of public social services who could build public consensus and consider the public interest. Previous illustrations of the attitude of Prime Minister Václav Klaus's government to tripartism, which precluded the signing of a General Agreement from 1995 to 1997, constitute further proof of this (see chapter 9). The logical first step would be to create such mechanisms.

Secondly, as far as freedom of information is concerned:

The Constitutional Charter of basic rights and freedoms directly states that government and self-government authorities "must provide information about their activities in a clear manner", and that a specific law should be passed to enumerate the details. However, no such law existed for a long time—the-only legal norm that addressed the right to information was a thirty-year-old law on the media. In a number of Anglo-Saxon countries a precept exists that requires civil servants to make available all information that is not legally designated 'secret'. To a government with the traditional Central European arrogance towards citizen appeals, something of this sort would be significant evidence that the army of civil servants is meant to serve citizens, rather than the other way around. (Kalous, 1996, 135)

A law binding government authorities to release to the public, on demand, all information concerning their activities, was passed as late as the spring of 1998 and will not take effect until 1999.

The function of individual ministries could be advantageously expanded to include a new dimension: the systematic support and stimulation of contacts and communication between participants, including representative groups of service providers and recipients. The openness of ministries to experts, the general public, and the media in the hectic times after the revolution in 1989 was exceptional in this sense and could serve as a model for the present.

The public has a better chance of being heard when citizens join forces within the framework of a civic association. The isolated voice of a single citizen, even when transmitted through the media, has never had enough political weight to force a large bureaucracy to consider it. Non-profit organizations are a promising means of presenting citizens' opinions and mediating dialogue between government and the public (see chapter 4).

Finally, in the course of their research on Czech public policy, experts have never doubted the independence of the media, although many have noted that media opinions tend to follow the currents of a particular political party or even the government. However, concern has been expressed regarding the distinct lack of depth or insight shown by journalists—illustrated, for example, by the press's sudden movement from extreme support for building funds and mortgages to a more critical and realistic approach (Valentová, 1995). Experts have also voiced dissatisfaction with the media's desire to attract readers at the expense of thorough analysis and warning citizens of important threats to their interests. This is particularly true in respect of crime (Cejp, 1995). Some have also complained openly about the lack of press interest in problems such as education reform (Kalous, 1995).

6. Opportunities for Experts to Influence the Formation and Implementation of Public Policy

Kalous (n.d., 1) poses the question: "How is it possible to promote expertise and continuity of action and implement long-term strategies in a democratic system? By definition, democracy encourages frequent changes of elected officials, therefore changing course is founded on wide participation and diverse interests. This makes aims difficult to achieve."

After the political changes in 1989, as in every revolutionary period, life was not complicated by procedural limits. It was a time in which specialists did not question anything, but rather entered politics. One example of this is the Program Commission of the Civic Forum movement. Many of its members were experts, and numerous personal unions and close friendships existed between the Commission and representative bodies of the newly constituted federal and national governments. Because of this, the political movement was provided with programmatic documents in the decisive months between November 1989 and June 1990 which formed a foundation for creating new laws and making fundamental executive decisions. The Program Commission of the Civic Forum was composed of more than ten specialized commissions. These commissions were in constant contact with each other by way of the common platform of the Program Commission and prepared not only programmatic documents in their own areas of expertise, but also a general program document—the Election Program of the Civic Forum.

The spontaneous, unmanaged, and unregulated entrance of specialists into policy formation had parallels within individual departments as well: ecologists played a significant role in preparing ecological laws in 1990–92; the group for housing reform, composed of academics, specialists, and representatives of key ministries, created the conception of housing policy in 1990 (Valentová, 1995); a working group for reform grew out of the Program Commission of the Civic Forum on health professionals in January 1990. This group prepared the first comprehensive proposal for reforming Czech health care, published in May 1990 (Proposal, 1990a). This formed the basis for the reform document "Proposal for a New System of Health Care" which was created by an editorial group composed of members of the working group and accepted by the Government of the Czech Republic in December 1990 (Proposal, 1990b); the Education Commission of the Civic Forum worked with student representatives on the wording of a new law on higher education. This law was accepted by the Federal Assembly as early as May 4, 1990.

During the chaotic times after the 1989 revolution, the necessary continuity of policy was also interrupted in ways that were detrimental to potentially functional and effective solutions. "In the hectic post-revolutionary period, there was a chance to promote and apply various particular, subjective, and voluntarist perspectives" (Kalous, 1995, 10).

The period beginning with the stable coalition government after the 1992 elections ushered in dramatically different forms of communication between experts and politicians. As the concrete examples which we shall put forward demonstrate, generally speaking, politicians grossly underestimated the importance of expert analysis in policy creation. Many politicians believed that ideological premises and clichés were sufficient to direct their decision-making. Another feature of the approach of politicians towards specialists was characterized by Sarvaš (1995, 115) as follows: "Some members of the highest leadership understood critical analysis as a threat to their power. Science, research, and analytical work were perceived as enemies of bureaucracy, as elements used to push it out of power."

In all too many departments and at many levels, self-interest, voluntarism, and dilettantism were widespread. However, few politicians in these departments were willing to concede that "reliance on common sense and experience does not guarantee that the required effects will be attained, because it introduces the danger of ineffective allocation of resources" (Sarvaš, 1995, 113).

Politicians' attitudes to ministerial research institutes are a good example of how they interpreted the analytic foundations of the formation and implementation of policy in their departments.

Housing Policy

Limited research capacity rendered the responsible Ministry of the Economy incapable of formulating effective arguments in favor of its proposed housing policies. Some research institutes dedicated to this issue were dismantled, including the Research Institute of Building and Architecture, while others were privatized. Research institutes that survived the restructuring are in a difficult position. They are scattered at separate universities and are not kept abreast of developments, plans, or trends in policy-making (Valentová, 1995, 20).

Defense

In 1993 the Minister of Defense closed the two institutes that composed the analytical basis of his department: the Military Institute for Social Research and the Institute for Strategic Studies. A similar process of eliminating analytic capacity occurred in military schools as well. The entire process of analysis as a part of policy-making was neglected (Sarvaš, 1995, 114).

Health Care

After 1989 the Institute of Social Medicine and the Organization of Health Care served as the center of health policy research. In order to address the changing conditions and requirements of the period the Minister of Health allowed the Institute to research and complete a proposal on how to transform itself. However, not long after his appointment in 1992 a new Minister of Health took the drastic step of abolishing the Institute altogether. The next Minister stopped funding the National Center for Health Promotion immediately after he took office in 1995. This had been a modern research, methodological, and marketing center which, through effective communication with the public, had played an exceptionally positive role promoting health care and the prevention of illness.

Health insurance laws did not obligate insurers or health care providers to collect data on medical and preventive care, or to provide these data to the state administration. As a result, the Ministry of Health, the government's administrative representative in this field, does not have the analytic data necessary to create health policy. Moreover, in order to optimize the system of reimbursements for health care, the Ministry of Health would need analyses of outputs and expenses which were formerly conducted by the abovementioned institutions (Háva and Kružík, 1996, 16).

It is fair to say that the Ministry of Health effectively cut itself off (or allowed itself to be cut off) from information essential for both the elementary objective analysis of health policy and policy formation. Steps to improve this situation have not been taken, and the political will does not currently exist.

Education

The role of research in transforming the education system was also distinctly undervalued. The center of pedagogical research, the Pedagogical Institute of the Czech Academy of Sciences, was closed, and the budget of another center of pedagogical and pedagogical–psychological research was significantly reduced. Even the current system of financing institutions of higher education does not support pedagogical research. A worrying number of government representatives elected in 1992 believed that the education system could be transformed within a short period, without initiating substantial cooperation with experts or public debate. However, even in countries with developed systems it takes five to ten years to prepare comprehensive, realistic plans for education reform (Kalous, 1996, 117–18).

The fact that politicians may more easily incorporate particular personal or group interests into policy when they are not confronted with solid information or analysis goes a long way towards explaining their preference for more 'spontaneous' development. Without expert analysis and research such politicians are in an easier position: no one complicates their lives with evidence that shows the negative effects of policies they conceive or implement.

7. The Relationship between Power Politics and Merit-Oriented Policy-Making

There is a visible tension between policy as a struggle to gain and maintain power, and public policy as the process of satisfying the public interest; this is particularly apparent when one considers individual political agendas. This conflict is most prevalent during disjointed historical periods like the one Central and Eastern Europe is currently experiencing, and in strongholds of power—issues related to the army and law and order. The following examples briefly illustrate the risks of narrow party politics, and how the promotion of power politics can threaten to undermine important, merit-based policy solutions.

The Army

After 1989—and especially after 1992—the Czech army became a battlefield for the most powerful partisan and economic interests. As a result, the finding of solutions to topical problems within the army itself took a lower priority (Sarvaš, 1995; Rašek, 1995). One example of this was the unprecedented scrutiny of all enlisted soldiers which further deepened their social insecurity, leading to a massive spontaneous exodus of soldiers from the army and reduced interest in the profession. This screening was conducted by the ministry in an attempt to show its determination to purify the army of ideologically suspect personnel (Rašek, 1995, 16).

Law and Order

Politicization of the security sector and security services is a chronic problem. There have been efforts to control the security sector in terms of party and ideological interests, and by politicizing the police. One negative effect of this is that the security services have become obsessed by internal conflicts and problems rather than concentrating on becoming a more stable force and determining a proper response to accelerating crime rates and expanding organized crime (Gabal, 1994, 96, 103).

The secret and intelligence services were reorganized, in terms of both their size and their activities. The process of their disintegration was exceptionally politicized, seriously undermining both public trust in these services and their chance of finding professional co-workers and new recruits. Critical analysis of this sphere after November 1989 generally assumes its almost complete destruction (Gabal, 1994, 90).

What kinds of solutions have been proposed for these conflicts? Gabal (1994, 95) views the law and order policy situation as follows: "The key prerequisites for improving the situation are to stabilize the police and security components, depoliticize them, and prevent each new political leadership from reorganizing the system, and from making massive changes in personnel." Another requirement is the substantial opening up of policy-making to public scrutiny, not excluding strongholds of power. This is particularly important because, as Arendt (1975, 161) puts it, "power always starts where the public ends". These conclusions have indisputable merit not only in respect of law and order policy and the army, but also in areas where the tension between policy as a struggle to gain and retain power and public policy as a process of satisfying the public interest does not represent a direct threat.

8. Conclusion: The Role of Public Policy

Although public policy is powerful it is not all-powerful. Policy may inspire, create, and shape society, but it may not go beyond the bounds of the possible. One limit of public policy is the people: their beliefs and needs, the comforts they are willing to sacrifice and what for, the ways in which they are willing to ignore boundaries that separate them from others, and their readiness to join forces to contribute to the public good. "The greatest problems a nation must confront, including the destruction of the family and the evaporation of civic virtues, are problems in human behavior upon which government programs have little affect. Even so, government may provide people with some direction. Our problems are not symptoms, but causes. They are fundamental. The best way to resolve them is by changing human thinking, attitudes, and deeds" (Morris in Purdun, 1996).

T. G. Masaryk and other thinkers have drawn similar conclusions. In their view, the key to reforming public policy lies in people's behavior and in government taking responsibility for educating citizens—citizenship training in the best sense of the term.

Public policy can and should be a little ahead of the times. It should not inhibit development. On the contrary, it should inspire. The words and deeds of its representatives should lead citizens to a greater understanding of the needs of the community and increase their preparedness to dedicate their own time and energy to address these needs. This kind of policy cannot be achieved by utilizing cold technology or wielding executive power. This conception of policy entails forming a vision for the future, creating and implementing programs, calmly analyzing topical problems in society, and patiently and democratically seeking the best methods to solve them. Citizens and experts are partners with policy and policy is their partner. Everything which supports this broadly defined framework is legitimate. That is why so much depends on properly functioning government, the notion that the administration should serve the public, and development of the civic sector and its institutions. This type of policy could truly be called 'public policy'.

III. CONCLUSION

12. The 'Choice of Society' in the Czech Republic

> If it is safe to believe that the Czech Republic is now firmly grounded as a democratic state with a market economy, more subtle issues present themselves to us for consideration: What character will our democratic state have in the future, in which direction will we steer, what roles does that entail, what will the country promote and against what will it defend itself? So far we have considered the country's basic forms of political, spiritual, civic, and economic life. Now we must consider in greater detail its actual content and long-term prospects . . .
>
> *Václav Havel (1995)*

1. Introduction

What form should the Czech Republic take in the coming decades? Not everyone considers this to be a legitimate question. Neo-liberals believe that creating a vision for the future and formulating developmental tendencies in advance may have far-reaching negative consequences. They disdainfully call it 'social engineering' or the excessive attempt to determine a free society's actions beyond a natural order which stems from the competition of various partial interests within a defined institutional framework.

I cannot agree with this. I am convinced that the ability to look ahead, formulate goals, and search for optimal methods of achieving them is an important feature of intelligence that may benefit not only individuals, but society as a whole. (See Vernardskij's theory of the 'noosphere' or the teleonomic qualities of social wholes in Potůček (1988) for more on this topic.) This ability depends on how well a given society prepares itself for possible threats and whether it takes advantage of potential development opportunities, thus positively influencing its chances of survival.

> *Example:*
> One positive example in Central and Eastern Europe is the Department for Strategic Studies
> in Poland, which is headed by a member of the government.

The prospect of any democracy allowing itself to be forced into accepting one exclusive vision of the future does not concern me. Differing development projects will naturally be undertaken, whether they are called visions, programs, or strategies. However, at the national level society should find sufficient will and concentration to discuss possible visions and choose one that seems optimal from a developmental viewpoint—one that integrates richly structured social interests and at the same time has the public's decisive political support.

The first citizen of the Czech Republic, President Václav Havel, has begun this discussion. Unless we take the view that public affairs are somehow beyond us, we—the other citizens of the Czech Republic—should not let this challenge go by. However, no vision of the Czech society of the future has yet been operationalized in the form of a concrete long-term program. Formulated concepts remain general and represent the political–philosophical views or even ideological beliefs of their authors. Solid foundations for considering the future, developmental threats, and opportunities that would produce intellectually sound 'brain trusts' are all lacking. At the beginning of the transition there may have been an objective barrier: the necessity of a 'hands on' approach to accomplish one-off phases of transformation. In the second half of the 1990s, however, the situation has changed markedly. Central and Eastern Europe is more stable, and the need to establish a concentrated analytical and prognostic base is urgent and inescapable.[1]

The main object of the present work is to propose an explanatory framework that enables us to understand the problems of regulation in contemporary society, and to utilize this framework to analyze the development of postcommunist societies since 1989. This analysis, in common with any study worthy of the name, also offers explanations of current problems and ways in which they might be solved. I propose such an analysis as one possible response to the Czech President's suggested debate on the 'choice of society'. Furthermore, it is clear that this would be relevant not only for the Czech Republic, but also for other Central and Eastern European countries, as a way of discovering similarities and differences in the region.

2. Where We Have Come From

Everything seemed much easier in 1989 than it does today. This is understandable. After nearly a decade we are better able to perceive and comprehend the pressure of the inheritance that has governed our actions since that time—and which will fade away only very slowly. The functioning of government institutions and people's attitudes are likely to be more durable than anyone could have imagined. We are at last in a position to fully appreciate Dahrendorf's estimate that while political institutions may be altered in six months and economic institutions in six years, social relations and attitudes are likely to register significant changes only after sixty years.

As the years since 1989 have confirmed the market may act as an engine of change—it 'stirs up the waters'. At the same time, it seems clear that the Czech Republic is not a 'standard Western society', and that it will not be one for a long time. It is also clear that the uncritical integration of Western regulatory models into a society that is painfully recovering from past injuries may lead to a protracted crisis and the massive appearance of socially pathological phenomena, leading to marked social and economic losses. Like it or not, Czech society is and for a long time will remain different—in both positive and negative respects— from the societies which found themselves on the other side of the Iron Curtain after the Second World War. Clearly, this must have a significant impact on the functioning and interrelationships of the market, government, and the civic sector.

3. What We Are

Our current situation is characterized by deformed relationships and a lack of balance between the market, government, and the civic sector. Private ownership and market principles were established at a time when government and its authorities acted, for the most part, as they had in the past—the public administration proved incapable of adapting to the substantial changes in its mission, aims, and functions in time to avoid this situation. After nearly fifty years of devastation in respect of civic virtues and civil society in the Czech Republic (1938–45, 1948–89), the civic sector was more or less left to its own resources, and government consistently undermined it. Thus, it had insufficient internal resources to act self-confidently and proactively, even where it could and should have functioned better than the market or government. The result was excessive opportunities for socially pathological forms of regulation, such as corruption and the mafia.

The Czech Republic is now paying for its attempts to speed up economic transformation at any price: in many cases, the 'changes' are formal rather than real. The slow change in the nature of social relationships may be discerned in the fact that, whether it was the reformers' intention or not, numerous old power coalitions and structures remain in place, facelifts notwithstanding, having successfully adapted to the new conditions. The old social capital has simply been converted into economic capital.

As the highest representative of the executive in the Czech Republic for many years Václav Klaus was not in an easy position. He could not fire every civil servant because he did not have new, qualified people on hand to replace them. He did not want to lose control over rapidly moving and historically unprecedented processes. Many unknowns entered the game and administrative mechanisms were weak. Given these factors a strong central government might well have appeared to be the best means and guarantee of implementing the necessary reforms. Such centralism, however, can be counterproductive because it may easily repeat the mistakes of old communist centralism. It may not obtain sufficient corrective feedback or renewed public support, and may end up implementing such undemocratic practices as top-down management.

Example:

Analysts of political developments since 1989 cannot help but notice a number of similarities between the approach of Václav Klaus's neo-liberal government (1992–97) to various social issues and the policies of the previous regime. Such a comparison has limited explanatory power, in part because the country's basic orientation was different in the two periods, but also the Klaus government was still feeling its way and necessarily combined the old with the new. Nevertheless, what in these ideologically antithetical periods was similar in terms of political priorities and instruments?

Economic development was carried out at the expense of other sectors in society, especially the public sector. Of course, the regulatory means utilized to achieve this aim—with the exception of fiscal policy—were dramatically different.

The emphasis was placed on central government and there was a distinct distaste for institutions mediating between government and individuals (especially regional public administration and self-government, the civic sector, and corporatist institutions) and for viewing the public administration's role within the framework of public service.

The importance of expert analysis in policy formation was underestimated. Research potential in the Czech Republic after 1992 was lower than at the end of the 1960s and 1980s.

Ethics and values fundamental to society were undervalued. "The conformity . . . of the opinions of pseudo-liberals on our political scene . . . with communists is not at all accidental. They either cannot or do not want to understand that neo-liberalism as a value does not mean freedom from spiritual or moral principles, but rather that moral dimensions give liberalism meaning and purpose" (Novotný, 1995, 149).

These similarities in no way show that communist and postcommunist regimes are fundamentally similar. They are fundamentally different in terms of the democratic foundations of social life and the related systematic creation of a market economy. The abovementioned similarities relate to political priorities and methods of exercising political power. After communism, inherited institutions and stereotypes of administrative behavior survived in many cases, albeit for different purposes.

With the ongoing transformation of society, some initially instrumental aspects of exercising political power will gain importance—and will have increasing influence on the regime's legitimacy. If legitimacy is to be maintained, however, it is necessary to pay heed to the increasing similarity between the two periods. What the public was willing to tolerate in the first years of transformation may increasingly be regarded as inadequate emancipation from the political aims and authoritarian practices of the communist past.

The Czech people are aware of the weaknesses of postcommunist politics, deformed relationships, and the disproportion between the market, government, and the civic sector. Government's enfeebled state has resulted in rising crime, legislative weaknesses at the heart of the privatization process have manifested themselves in increasing corruption, and conflicts of public and private interests have led to the siphoning off of public funds. Problems associated with nearly all areas of the public sector (social security, care for families and children, housing, health care, education) are perceived as urgent. Systematic errors in the emerging market economy, in which the regulatory role of government was underestimated as seriously as in the sectors mentioned above, have recently been brought to the public's attention.

Neo-liberals consider their primary political aim to be the maximization of the role of the market in society. This concept, however, introduced in practice at the beginning of the nineteenth century, does not address the needs of contemporary society and cripples government and the civic sector: "There is one-sidedness and political immaturity in the political elite's conception of the non-economic dimensions of transformation. They take a pragmatic economic and empirical view of the legislative process and undermine the political process through narrow party interests. In the end, this results in the degradation of politics and civic life [for the benefit of] economic transformation . . ." (Gabal, 1996, 6).

The neglected role of government since 1989 has forced the Czech Republic to rely consistently on the state apparatus, whose organizational structure, functioning, and work stereotypes were in many respects inherited from communism.

The perceived role of various regulators in contemporary Czech society has also affected the government's position towards civic sector institutions. The law on non-profit associations was not passed until 1995, after many delays and useless procrastination. The law on foundations did not get through Parliament until the end of 1996. Non-profit organizations were given no grounds to believe that they had the necessary support from Klaus's government to tackle the tasks that stood before them.

In short, in many ways neither Czech citizens nor their political representatives were able to emerge from the shadow of the past. Václav Klaus's key political slogan in 1995, to the effect that the Czech Republic had completed its transformation to a market economy and a standard European democracy, must be catalogued with other statements generated rather as momentary political propaganda than as realistic evaluations of the actual situation. Now our prime concern must be to concentrate on the real problems society is facing and how they may be solved.

4. Where We Are Going

I propose the following thesis: the transformation of postcommunist societies and their rebirth as decent and civilized communities is a long-term process. Economists do not expect stabilized ownership relationships in the Czech Republic prior to 2005; reform of public administration has not yet begun; the civic sector is only now beginning to stand on its own feet and find its proper place between government and the market; and only twenty per cent of citizens trust the Parliament, whereas three out of four associate wealth with dishonesty. These facts illustrate that we are still only at the beginning of transformation, and that a long and arduous road stretches before us. It is difficult to foresee the end of this process when social reality is changing before our eyes, advanced Western countries are facing serious problems and seeking new solutions, and there are few concrete criteria or firm points on which we can depend with assurance.

Preoccupation with our own problems should not prevent us from recognizing that there will also be changes in external conditions. On the positive side, in an international political perspective it seems that the Czech Republic's position will not be seriously threatened in the coming years. Even so, the globalization of the world economy is constantly putting greater pressure on the efficiency of the Czech economy. The process of integration into the European Union requires an ability to adapt to many distinct and complex norms and institutional environments, including supranational forms of regulation. The information society and differentiation of lifestyles demands new ways in which social interests may be represented. New forms of social tension will result as the social stratification created by the industrial epoch is replaced by a new, more fluid society.

Two scenarios for the future development of the Czech Republic are foreseeable and can be interpreted as opposites.

The first scenario will result if neither citizens nor their political representatives find sufficient strength to react adequately to the challenges of the time. That would lead to a consistent reduction in government authority and legitimacy, a degeneration of institutions of civil society, and a poorly functioning economy trailing behind world technological developments. There would also be more scope for the appearance of destructive, socially pathological phenomena. The result of such a scenario would be a chronic protracted crisis, not dissimilar to what happened in Bulgaria in the mid-1990s.

The second scenario incorporates conclusions that were accepted at a meeting of experts dedicated to the development of public administration which took place during the Fiftieth General Assembly of the United Nations (Public Administration, 1996). It would depend upon the recognition by decisive political forces and representatives of civil society of the importance of formulating a long-term development strategy for the Czech Republic and its systematic and public discussion, cultivation, and gradual implementation. Any such vision would have to overcome the limitations placed on it by party ideology. Its formulation would require a social contract between social actors identifying the country's basic problems and methods for solving them—similar to what the Czech Republic experienced after the revolution in 1989.

Based on the discussions contained in this study, and without claiming to address every issue fully, let me conclude by listing the elements that should on no account be overlooked in the development of such a long-term strategy.

The overarching aims of Czech society and government must be formulated. Beyond the advantages and disadvantages of the available regulatory mechanisms for the 'choice of society', I would emphasize the need to expand opportunities for cultivating and utilizing human potential in all the basic functional areas of individual life: as a person, as a member of a family, region and greater society, and as a creator of material and spiritual values (within the framework of care for the environment and cultural traditions). Beyond these basic elements, the overarching aims of Czech society should be to uphold the following principles: protection of human rights, including the right to a dignified existence, sustainable development, and shared responsibility for the fate of Europe and humankind.

Considerations of the relationship between the market, government, and the civic sector should be politically mediated. No regulator should be prioritized at the expense of the others. On the contrary, methods should be found that allow the capabilities of each to be optimally utilized, and their mutual cooperation should be supported in order to allow them to supplement one another synergistically. This would require a new definition of the role and function of government in a continuously changing political and economic context.

Public administration should be reformed. It should be depoliticized, the state administration professionalized, and the prestige of civil servants raised. This could be accomplished by means of legislation on the civil service, establishing a code of proper public administration, instituting internal control mechanisms, substituting a hierarchical approach with one that promotes partnership with citizens, and enforcing the Freedom of Information Act (which only protects government information that truly needs to remain confidential).

The establishment of regional self-government should be implemented, allowing it to become a regular part of public administration.

The quality of the preventive, control, and repressive functions of public administration—especially the courts and the police—should be radically improved. This should focus on reducing crime, fighting corruption and organized crime, upholding a legal framework for the privatization process, and depriving illegal activities of capital resources.

The importance of the public sector should be fully recognized. Systematic work should be conducted to find new methods of administration and financing, including the establishment of a mechanism to link wage increases in the public sector with those in the private sphere. Various forms of competitive cooperation between the public and private sectors should be instituted.

Functional and effective methods for the engagement of government in the market economy should be established.

The civic sector should be provided with opportunities to develop, and its development should be actively encouraged by all appropriate legislative means and financial stimuli. These could include supporting citizen participation in public affairs, strengthening corporatist elements such as tripartism and para-fiscal funds, and facilitating other forms of long-term cooperation between public administration and the civic sector.

Informal, but more systematic and consistent civic education should be established and incorporated in all relevant educational contexts and methodologies.

In the end, the 'choice of society' in a democracy is the right of citizens. They decide which vision of the future will be given preference, and through their actions they either support it or prefer another, competing idea.

Without the mediating role of public policy, however, citizens themselves are unable to achieve their goals. Responsible public policy can grasp the extent to which it is possible to overcome the everyday worries that occupy public consciousness, precisely comprehend the needs of the times, integrate the call of social conscience, stimulate development, inspire people to extraordinary actions, and prepare them for tasks that will emerge in the future. It can. If only it could: whether it will in fact be able to depends on us—the citizens.

APPENDIX

The Disciplinary Foundations of the Present Study

The writing of the present study was influenced by a number of disciplines and spiritual traditions.

Lindblom (1977) and Wallerstein (1979) agree that contemporary thought is still influenced by the liberal thought of the nineteenth century which split the problems of contemporary societies into three main categories: (i) economics, or the market; (ii) political science and the law, or the government; and (iii) sociology, which analyzes civil society.

This was not always the case: the classical political economy of the eighteenth century did not distinguish between political and economic perspectives. These two main streams of liberal thinking were constituted after the French Revolution—the first concerned with analyzing government and the other with analyzing the market, both as regulators of public life. The usefulness of breaking down analyses of the market, politics, and even society became widespread and now is almost never challenged.

This specialization and separation of work has undoubtedly brought great results in the social sciences. On the other hand, this approach has deprived us of a holistic framework for understanding society and the way it influences our lives. As point of departure I have used Wallerstein's assumption that various accepted and applied social sciences are not specific disciplines, in the sense of coherent object-focused pursuits organized around either discreet degrees of generalization or meaningful elements of analysis. Rather these disciplines have the same object—human society. It is convenient to separate these disciplines in order to solve particular tasks of cognition or for organizational purposes, but not to affect cognitive goals as such, nor to construct universal explanatory theories. As Wallerstein (1979) puts it: "The borders among disciplines do not make sense from an intellectual point of view, but only from a pragmatic point of view."

The method which I have generally applied in this book is the parallel use of different abstractions. Each abstraction describes only a small part of the social whole unless related to others. When we search for these relations, we attain a more complex, though still limited, description and understanding of the problems of contemporary societies.

This approach is not only ambitious, but also very risky. However, my efforts are buttressed by the thoughts and analyses of many authors who have taken this dangerous path in previous decades. Only through continual cultivation of an interdisciplinary approach is it possible to avoid the many painful errors and disappointments that result from the uncritical application of incomplete explanatory frameworks to resolve global practical problems. "If we are to act in the world rather than only investigate, we have to consider it in the way it is, i.e., with its whole complexity, and we have to cope with all the important determinants, conditions and influences. In this case, the complex paradigms are more efficient than those which are too concentrated and economical" (Etzioni, 1995, 237–38).

A particularly important element of my approach in the present study is sociology, a social science broad enough to encompass important aspects of social change. Equally important is the young and flexible science known as public policy, which uses the frameworks of economics, political science, law, sociology, anthropology, and other disciplines to analyze the processes of forming and implementing solutions to specific social problems while taking due note of the public interest. It focuses particularly on the analysis of the institutional mediation of these processes to the public, civic, and, to a certain extent, private sectors in a manner useful to policy-making (Potůček et al., 1994). Other relevant disciplines include administrative science, organizational theory, and information science.

I agree with Václav Klaus that "a clear theoretical conception is a necessary compass for our behavior and—in the same way as sailors of old—we are unable to act without it" (Klaus, 1996, 333). However, I perceive the complexity of the social sciences, which collaborate to describe current society, differently to Klaus: "Social sciences—and especially the 'hardest' and most elaborate one, economics—are indispensable in creating visions" (ibid., 332). This argument risks overemphasizing one discipline at the expense of others, what the American sociologist Fritz recently called "the arrogant colonization of the social sciences by economics".

ENDNOTES

Preface to the Czech Edition
1. In the European sense of the term.

Chapter 5
1. Compare, for example, Results (1995), Potůček (1997), and Purkrábek et al. (1996).
2. Compare Purkrábek et al. (1996, 25) and the research conducted by IVVM and STEM in 1996.

Chapter 6
1. See, for example, Lukes (1992). A more detailed discussion of the relationship between freedom and equality has been started by Potůček (1995b).

Chapter 7
1. For a more detailed discussion of the functioning and problems of welfare states, see Potůček (1995) and Večeřa (1993).

Chapter 8
1. See for instance Batt (1991), Brom and Orenstein (1993), Earle, Frydman, Rapaczynski, and Turkewitz (1994), Ježek (1993), Mejstřik et al.(1997), Mlčoch (1994, 1996, 1997), Možný et al.(1995), Rychetský (1995), Švejnar (1993), and *The Privatization Newsletter of the Czech Republic and Slovakia,* published by the Institute of Economic Studies at the Faculty of Social Sciences, Charles University, Prague. This chapter incorporates these sources, as well as materials from newspapers and magazines.

Chapter 9
1. The 'prisoner's dilemma' describes a situation in which one actor's decision is based on his assumptions concerning how another actor will act and vice-versa, without the possibility of negotiating the decision in advance. If both trust that the other will act co-operatively, they both gain. If they do not trust each other, they still gain, but not as much. If one actor expects the other's cooperation and acts accordingly, but in the event the other feels unable to do so, the former faces the worst scenario of all and the latter the best.
2. This section is based on a study by Wilensky and Turner (1987).
3. This section is based primarily on analyses published by Orenstein (1994) and Mansfeldová (1994a, 1994b) and information from the daily press.
4. These thoughts continue a discussion I began in the Czech daily newspapers *MF Dnes* and *Lidové Noviny* in 1995–96 concerning the problems and functions of corporatism in the Czech Republic. Václav Bělohradský and Lubomír Brokl contributed the other side of the dialogue.

Chapter 11
1. Potůček et al. (1994; 1995; 1996), and Purkrábek et al. (1996).

Chapter 12

1. In March 1998 an international conference, "Czech Society at the End of the Millennium", was organized at the Faculty of Social Sciences at Charles University in Prague. Possible visions of the Czech state were extensively discussed, encompassing a wide range of dimensions: social, political, institutional, economic, and ecological (see Potůček, 1999).

BIBLIOGRAPHY

Alan, J. et al. (1989). *Koncepce rodinné politiky* (Family Policy Conception). Project. Prague: Research Institute of Social Development and Work.

Arendt, H. (1975). *Elemente und Ursprünge totaler Herrschaft*. Band III. Ullstein Buch.

Archer, R. (1994). *Markets and Good Government*. Geneva: United Nations Non-Governmental Liaison Service.

Arrow, K. J. (1971). *Společenský výběr a individuální hodnoty* (Social choice and individual values). Prague: Svoboda.

―――. (1974). *The Limits of Organization*. New York: W. W. Norton.

Baker, R. (1993). "Democracy versus Bureaucracy: Transformation and the Civil Service in Bulgaria." Unpublished essay.

Barry, N. (1987). "Understanding the Market." In *The State or the Market*, ed. M. Loney. London: Sage.

Batt, J. (1991). *Economic Reform and Political Change in Eastern Europe: A Comparison of the Czech and Hungarian Experience*. New York: Council of Foreign Relations Press.

Bělohradský, V. (1996). "Luxova cesta ke korporativnímu státu" (Lux's path to a corporatist state). *Lidové noviny* 9 (15 April): 6.

Brokl, L. (1995). *Institucionalizace zájmů v české společnosti* (The institutionalization of interests in Czech society). Unpublished manuscript, Sociological Institute, Prague.

Brom, K., and M. Orenstein (1993). *The 'Privatized Sector' in the Czech Republic: Government and Bank Control in a Transitional Economy*. Prague: Institute for East–West Studies.

Brown, B. (1994). "Unbalanced Sectoral Development in the Czech Republic: Democracy and the Civic, Market, and State Sectors." Unpublished manuscript, Charles University, Prague.

Brzezinski, Z. (1993). *Bez kontroly. Chaos v předvečer 21. století* (Out of control: Chaos on the eve of the 21st century). Prague: Victoria Publishing.

Čapek, K. (1993). *O věcech obecných čili zóon politikon* (On public affairs or 'zoon politikon'). Prague: Melantrich.

Cejp, M. (1995). *Kriminalita v České republice po roce 1989 a společenská protiopatřen.* (Crime in the Czech Republic after 1989 and social counter-measures) Internal study, Institute of Sociological Studies, Faculty of Social Sciences, Charles University, Prague.

Dahrendorf, R. (1985). *Law and Order*. London.

Damohorský, M. (1995). *Vývojové tendence Českého svazu ochránců přírody* (Developmental tendencies of the Czech Association for the Protection of Nature). Internal study, Institute of Sociological Studies, Faculty of Social Sciences, Charles University, Prague.

Drucker, P. (1993). *Postkapitalistická společnost* (Postcapitalist society). Prague: Management Press.

———. (1994). *Věk diskontinuity* (The age of discontinuity). Prague: Management Press.

Earle, J. S., R. Frydman, A. Rapaczynski, and J. Turkewitz (1994). *Small Privatization*. Budapest: CEU Press.

Etzioni, A. (1991). "Eastern Europe: The Wealth of Lessons." *Challenge* (July–August).

———. (1995). *Morální dimenze ekonomiky*. Prague: Victoria Publishing. Czech translation of *The Moral Dimension: Towards a New Economics*. New York: The Free Press, 1988.

Frič, P. et al. (1996). *Neziskový sektor v ČR* (The non-profit sector in the Czech Republic). Unpublished study, Faculty of Social Sciences, Charles University, Prague.

Friedman, M., and R. Friedman (1980). *Free to Choose*. London: Secker and Warburg.

Fromm, E. (1994). *Mít nebo být?* (To have or to be?). Prague: Naše vojsko.

Fukuyama, F. (1995). *Trust: The Social Virtues and the Creation of Prosperity*. London: Hamish Hamilton.

Gabal, I. (1994). "Občanská společnost nebo trh bezpečnosti" (Civil society, or The market with safety). *Listy* 14, No. 2: 83–96.

———. (1996). Dvě koncepce transformace—spor o kvalitu české budoucnosti (Two conceptions of transformation—Controversies about the quality of the Czech future). Prague: Institute for East–West Studies.

Gál, F., ed. (1994). *Násilí* (Violence). Prague: EGEM.

Gambetta, D. (1993). *The Sicilian Mafia. The Business of Private Protection*. Cambridge, MA, and London: Harvard University Press.

Háva, P., and L. Kružík (1995). "Průběh privatizace v českém zdravotnictví" (The story of privatization in Czech health care), *in Analýza událostí veřejné politiky v České republice* (An analysis of public policy events in the Czech Republic), M. Potůček et al., Vol. 1, Public and Social Policy Series (February 1995), 54–76. Prague: Institute of Sociological Studies, Faculty of Social Sciences, Charles University.

———. (1996). *Veřejnoprávní zdravotní pojištění v ČR v letech 1991–95* (Public health insurance in the Czech Republic, 1991–95). Internal study, Institute of Sociological Studies, Faculty of Social Sciences, Charles University, Prague.

Havel, V. (1995). "Jedna etapa končí—co tedy bude dál?" (One epoch is ending—What comes next?). Speech given to the Chamber of Deputies in the Parliament of the Czech Republic. *Lidové noviny* 8 (15 March): 7–9.

Hayek, F. A. (1976). *Law, Legislation and Liberty*. Vol. 2, *The Mirage of Social Justice*. Chicago and London: University of Chicago Press.

Hendrych, D. (1992). *Základy správní vědy* (The basics of public administration). Prague: Aleko.

Hesse, J. J. (1993). "From Transformation to Modernization: Administrative Change in Central and Eastern Europe." *Public Administration* 21, No. 1/2: 219–57.

Hirschman, A. O. (1970). *Exit, Voice and Loyalty*. Cambridge: Harvard University Press.

Jařab, J. (1996). "Básníků není nikdy dost" (There are never enough poets). *Magazín Dnes* (4 July): 28–30.

Ježek, T. (1993). *Privatizace a Fond národního majetku* (Privatization and the National Property Fund). Prague: CERGE.

K výsledkům výzkumu názorů občanů České republiky na veřejnou politiku (Results of research on public opinion concerning public policy in the Czech Republic) (1995). Prague: Institute of Sociological Studies, Faculty of Social Sciences, Charles University.

Kalous, J. (1995). "Hlavní problémy vzdělávací politiky České republiky v transformačním období" (The main problems of education policy in the Czech Republic in the period of transformation), in *Analýza událostí veřejné politiky v České republice* (An analysis of public policy events in the Czech Republic), M. Potůček et al., Vol. 1, Public and Social Policy Series (February 1995), 77–95.

———. (n.d.). *Vzdělávací politika* (Education policy). Unpublished manuscript.

———. (1996). *Vzdělávací politika* (Education policy). Doctoral thesis, Pedagogical Faculty, Charles University, Prague.

Kameníček, J., and K. Kouba, eds. (1992). *Trh versus plán—půl století sporů* (The market versus the plan—A half century of contention). Prague: Karolinum.

Kjarum, M. (1992). "The Contributions of Voluntary Organizations to the Development of Democratic Governance." *In The Role of Voluntary Organizations in Emerging Democracies*. Report from a workshop at the Czechoslovak Management Center, Čelákovice, Czech Republic.

Klaus, V. (1996). *Mezi minulostí a budoucností* (Between the past and the future). Brno and Prague: Jan Masaryk Foundation/Georgetown and Svoboda.

Kolarska-Bobinska, L. (n.d.) *The Role of the State in the Transitional Period*. Unpublished manuscript.

Kornai, J. (1990). *Vision and Reality, Market and State*. New York: Harvester Wheatsheaf.

Lane, J. E. (1993). *The Public Sector. Concepts, Models and Approaches*. London: Sage.

Lehmbruch, G., and P. S. Schmitter, eds. (1982*). Patterns of Corporatist Policy-Making*. London: Sage.

Lindblom, C. E. (1977). *Politics and Markets*. New York: Basic Books.

Lukes, S. (1992). *On Trade-Offs between Values*. EUI Working Paper No. 92/24. Florence: European University Institute.

Majone, G. (1994). "The Emergence of the Regulatory State." Lecture given at the conference 'Institutional Change in Europe', Oxford University.

Mannheim, K. (1991). *Ideologie a utopie.* (Ideology and utopia) Bratislava: Archa.

Manning, N., T. H. Marshall, and J. Habermas (1993). "Citizenship and Transition in Eastern Europe." *World Development* 21, No. 8: 1313–28.

Mansfeldová, Z. (1994a). "Tripartism in the Czech Political System." Paper prepared for the workshop 'Common Features of East and Central European Transformations', Berlin.

———— (1994b). "Tripartism in the Czech Republic." Paper prepared for the roundtable conference 'Tripartism in Central and Eastern Europe', Budapest.

Marshall, T. H. (1963). *Sociology at the Crossroads.* London: Heinemann.

Mejstřík, M., ed. (1997). *The Privatization Process in East-Central Europe: Evolutionary Process of Czech Privatizations.* Dordrecht, Boston, and London: Kluwer Academic Publishers.

Mishan, E. J. (1981). *Introduction to Normative Economics.* Oxford: Oxford University Press.

Mlčoch, L. (1994). "Restrukturalizace vlastnických vztahů očima institucionálního ekonoma" (Restructuring of ownership relations from the viewpoint of an institutional economist). Lecture delivered during professorial appointment proceedings, Faculty of Social Sciences, Charles University, Prague.

————. (1996). "Czech Privatization—Penalties for Speed." Unpublished manuscript, Institute of Economic Studies, Faculty of Social Sciences, Charles University, Prague.

————. (1997). *Institucionální ekonomie* (Institutional economics). Prague: Karolinum.

Moe, R. C. (1987). "Exploring the Limits of Privatization." *Public Administration Review* 47, No. 6: 453–60.

Možný, I. (1991). *Proč tak snadno?* (Why so easy?) Prague: Sociological Publishing House.

Možný, I. et al. (1995). *The Social Consequences of Changes in Ownership.* Brno: Masaryk University, Philosophical Faculty, No. 306.

Munková, G. (1996). *Vývoj sociální politiky ve vztahu k rodině* (The development of social policy related to families). Internal study, Institute of Sociological Studies, Faculty of Social Sciences, Charles University, Prague.

Musil, J. (1996). "Nový pohled na občanskou společnost" (A new view on civil society). *The New Presence* 2, No. 1: 31.

Myrdal, G. (1968). *Asian Drama: An Inquiry into the Poverty of Nations.* Harmondsworth: Pelican Books.

Naisbitt, J., and P. Aburdenová (1992). *Megatrendy 2000* (Megatrends 2000). Bratislava: Bradlo.

Novotný, F. (1995). "Obnova neziskových organizací církví a náboženských společenství v ČR" (Reviving religious non-profit organizations and societies in the Czech Republic), *in Analýza událostí veřejné politiky v České republice* (An analysis of public policy events in the Czech Republic), M.

Potůček et al., Vol. 1, Public and Social Policy Series (February 1995), 138–58.

Nozick, R. (1974). *Anarchy, State and Utopia.* Oxford: Basil Blackwell.

Okun, A. M. (1975). *Equality and Efficiency: The Big Tradeoff.* Washington: The Brookings Institute.

Orenstein, M. (1994). "The Czech Tripartite Council and its Contribution to Social Peace." Paper presented at the Third Prague Workshop on Social Responses to Economic Transformation, Central European University, Prague.

Osborne, D., and T. Gaebler (1992). *Reinventing Government. How the Entrepreneurial Spirit is Transforming the Public Sector.* Reading: Addison-Wesley Publishing Co.

Popper, K. R. (1994). *Otevřená společnost a její nepřátelé* (The open society and its enemies). Prague: ISE.

———. (1995). *Věčné hledání. Intelektuální autobiografie* (The eternal search: An intellectual autobiography). Prague: Vesmír.

Potůček, M. (1988). "A Teleonomic Explanatory Scheme." *World Futures* 25, No. 1: 1–11.

———. (1991). "Pojetí lidského potenciálu" (The concept of human potential). *Psychologie v ekonomické praxi* 26, No. 3: 115–24.

———. (1992). "The Concept of Human Potential and Social Policy." *Acta Universitatis Carolinae Oeconomica* 1: 51–67.

———. (1994a). *Transformace zdravotní péče v České republice v letech, 1990–1992* (The transformation of health care in the Czech Republic 1990–92). Prague: Nadace START (Start Foundation).

———. (1994b). "Trh a správa v teorii a praxi sociální transformace" (Market and government in the theory and practice of societal transformation). *Sociologický časopis* 30, No. 1: 43–50.

———. (1995a). "Faktory, kritéria a problémy sociální reformy" (Factors, criteria, and problems of social reform), *in Analýza událostí veřejné politiky v České republice*, M. Potůček et al., Vol. I, Public and Social Policy Series (February 1995), 16–35.

———. (1995b). *Sociální politika* (Social policy). Prague: Sociological Publishing House.

———. (1997). "How Czechs reflect the tasks and transformation of the public sector." In *Developing Organizations and Changing Attitudes: Public Administration in Central and Eastern Europe*, ed. J. Jabes, 171–81. Bratislava, The Network of Institutes and Schools of Public Administration in Central and Eastern Europe (NISPAcee).

Potůček, M. ed. (1999). *Česká společnost na konci tisíciletí* (Czech society at the end of the millennium). Proceedings of an international conference organized by the Faculty of Social Sciences, Charles University, Prague, on the occasion of the 600th anniversary of Charles University, 12–14 March 1998. Prague: Karolinum.

Potůček, M. et al. (1994). *Zrod teorie veřejné politiky v České republice* (The birth of public policy theory in the Czech Republic). Public and Social Policy

Series (January 1994). Prague: Institute of Sociological Studies, Faculty of Social Sciences, Charles University.

———. (1995). *Analýza událostí veřejné politiky v České republice* (An analysis of public policy events in the Czech Republic), Vol. I, Public and Social Policy Series (February 1995). Prague: Institute of Sociological Studies, Faculty of Social Sciences, Charles University.

———. (1996). *Analýza událostí veřejné politiky v České republice* (An analysis of public policy events in the Czech Republic), Vol. II, Public and Social Policy Series (March 1996). Prague: Institute of Sociological Studies, Faculty of Social Sciences, Charles University.

Proposal for Reforming Health Care (Návrh reformy péče o zdraví) (1990a). Prague: Working group for reform, the Ministry of Health of the Czech Republic.

Proposal for a New System of Health Care (Návrh nového systému zdravotní péče) (1990b). Prague: Ministry of Health of the Czech Republic.

Public Administration and Development (1996). Resumed Fiftieth General Assembly Session. New York, United Nations.

Purdun, T. S. (1996). "Facts of Clinton." *The New York Times Magazine* (19 May).

Purkrábek, M. et al. (1996). *Občan a veřejná politika* (The citizen and public policy). Prague: Faculty of Social Sciences, Charles University.

Rašek, A. (1995). *Transformace personální struktury armády* (Transforming the personnel structure of the army). Internal study, Institute of Sociological Studies, Faculty of Social Sciences, Charles University, Prague.

Rausser, G. C., and S. R. Johnson (1993). "State–market–civil institutions: The case of Eastern Europe and the Soviet Republics." *World Development* 21, No. 4: 675–89.

Ringen, S. (1987) *The Possibility of Politics.* Oxford: Clarendon Press.

Roebroek, J. M. (1992). *The Imprisoned State.* Unpublished manuscript, Tilburg University.

Rose, R., and C. Haerpfer (1992). *New Democracies between State and Market. Studies in Public Policy* No. 204. Glasgow: Center for the Study of Public Policy, University of Strathclyde.

Rose, R. (1996). "Trust and Distrust for Emerging Civil Society." Conference paper, Tirana, NISPAcee Conference.

Rychetský, P. (1995). "Odvrácená tvář české privatizace" (The other side of Czech privatization). *Hospodářské noviny* 1 and 2 (10–11 May).

Sarvaš, Š. (1995). "Profesionalizace armády jako problém veřejného zájmu" (Voluntary service in the army as an issue of the public interest), in *Analýza událostí veřejné politiky v České republice*, M. Potůček et al., Vol. I, Public and Social Policy Series (February 1995), 96–116.

Sen, A. (1984). *Resources, Values and Development.* Oxford: Basil Blackwell.

———. (1990). "Individual Freedom as a Social Commitment." *New York Review of Books* (14 June).

Shleifer, A. (1994). *Establishing Property Rights.* Proceedings of Annual Conference on Development Economics. Washington: The World Bank.

Schöpflin, G. (1991). "Postcommunist Constituting New Democracies in Central Europe." *International Affairs* 67, No. 2: 235–50.

Sojka, M., and B. Konečný (1996). *Malá encyklopedie moderní ekonomie* (A small encyclopedia of modern economics). Prague: Libri.

Soros, G. (1991). *Směnka na demokracii* (Bill of democracy). Prague: Prostor.

Spiazzi, R. (1993). *Sociální kodex církve* (Catholic social teachings). Tišnov, Czech Republic: Sursum.

Státní politika životního prostředí (Government environmental policy) (1995). Prague: Ministry of the Environment of the Czech Republic.

Streeck, W., and P.C. Schmitter (1985*). Private Interest Government. Beyond Market and State.* London: Sage.

Streeten, P. (1989). *Mobilizing Human Potential. The Challenge of Unemployment.* New York: United Nations Development Program.

————. (1993). "Markets and States." *World Development* 21, No. 8: 1281–98.

Šilhánová, H. et al. (1996). *Základní informace o neziskovém sektoru v ČR* (Basic information about the non-profit sector in the Czech Republic). Prague: Civil Society Development Foundation.

Švejnar, J. (1993). *Historie a současnost československé privatizace* (History and the present in Czechoslovak privatization). Prague: CERGE.

Tawney, R. H. (1952). *The Acquisitive Society.* London: G. Bell and Sons.

"Teze k programu zdraví" (Theses about the health program) (1990). *Zdravotnické noviny* 29, No. 4 (26 January).

Ticháček, B. (1995). "Reforma sféry péče o veřejné zdraví" (Reform of public health), in *Analýza událostí veřejné politiky v České republice,* M. Potůček et al., Vol. I, Public and Social Policy Series (February 1995), 36–53.

Uphoff, N. (1993). "Grassroots Organizations and NGOs in Rural Development: Opportunities with Diminishing States and Expanding Markets." *World Development* 21, No. 4: 607–22.

Valentová, B. (1995). *Politika bydlení po roce 1989* (Housing policy after 1989). Internal study, Institute of Sociological Studies, Faculty of Social Sciences, Charles University, Prague.

Vavroušek, J. (1993). "Závod s časem. Hledání lidských hodnot slučitelných s trvale udržitelným způsobem života" (A race against time. Searching for human values that are compatible with a sustainable way of life*). Literární noviny* 4, No. 49 (9 December): 1, 3.

Večeřa, M. (1993). *Sociální stát* (The Welfare State). Prague: Sociological Publishing House.

Vidláková, O. (1995). "The Path of Public Administration Reform and Internationalization in the Czech Republic." *Public Management Forum 1,* No. 4: 10–11.

Vozar, D. (1996). "The Czech Non-Profit Sector in Theory and Practice." Thesis, Faculty of Social Sciences, Charles University, Prague.

Wallerstein, I. (1979). *The Capitalist World-Economy.* Cambridge: Cambridge University Press.

Weigle, M.A., and J. Butterfield (1993). "Civil Society in Reforming Communist Regimes." *Comparative Politics* 25, No. 2: 1–23.

Weimer, D. L., and A. R. Vining (1992). *Policy Analysis. Concepts and Practice.* Englewood Cliffs: Prentice Hall.

Wildavsky, A. (1980). *How to Limit Government Spending.* Berkeley: University of
        California Press.
Wilensky, H. L., and L. Turner. (1987). *Democratic Corporatism and Policy Linkages.*
        Research Series No. 69. Berkeley: University of California, Institute of
        International Studies.
Wolfenden Commission (1978). *The Future of Voluntary Organizations. Report of the
        Wolfenden Commission.* London: Croom Helm.